Women Who Lead

Stories about women who are making a difference

Yong Hui V. McDonald

1. Leadership
2. Inspirational
3. Women

"I AM THE LIGHT OF THE WORLD."

(John 9:5B)

Dedication

I dedicate this book to our Heavenly Father, our Lord Jesus, the Holy Spirit, and all the people who have the desire to lead and to learn how to lead.

Acknowledgments

My gratitude to all the authors who contributed their stories for this book, Holly Weipz who drew a beautiful illustrations, and Regina Fernandez, Mike Goins, Laura Nokes Lang, Lynette McClain, Cathy Oasheim, Sunmin Park, Doug Purdy, and Sam Rodriguez for editing.

Contents

Dedication

Acknowledgments

Introduction

1. "Following My Heart"
   By Maxine Morarie / 13

2. "Everything Is a Learning Experience"
   By Laura Nokes Lang / 29

3. "Arising Dreams"
   By Angela McMahan / 45

4. "Making a Difference"
   By Sung Hea Rhim / 63

5. "Tough Lessons"
   By Lynette McClain / 77

6. "Able to See Solutions"
  By Gael Sylvia Pullen / 99

7. "Privilege and Honor to Lead"
  By Reverend Edna Morgan / 113

8. "Giver of the Vision"
  By Yong Hui V. McDonald / 131

Appendices

An Invitation / 150
Resources:
Transformation Project Prison Ministry / 151
Heaven's Gate Ministry / 152
Veterans Twofish Foundation / 153
About The Author
About The Illustrator

Introduction

A while back, the Lord asked me to write a book to help future leaders, so I have been thinking about writing a book on leadership; but this book is not what I had in mind at all. However, I believe this book was not an accident. It was the Lord's plan to get many of His dedicated servants' stories out to the world to encourage and inspire future leaders.

One Sunday, the Lord asked me to visit New Gate Church in Denver, a Korean church that supports Transformation Project Prison Ministry (TPPM). I asked Him why He wanted me to go there, and He told me that someone that I should meet would be at the church. I went to New Gate, and before the worship service began, I spent time with a seminary student. She told me she was having difficulty finding resources for writing a research paper on women in leadership. We checked the church library, but we couldn't find any English or Korean books on the subject.

I reflected on this incident. There are many amazing women leaders who are making a difference in the world, but we rarely hear or read their stories.

How can we teach and inspire young women to become leaders if women leaders do not share their histories? So, I decided to gather stories of women who are making a difference in the church and in the community for this book project. After I started this project, the Lord asked me to approach specific people to discuss writing their stories for this book. It became apparent to me that the Lord was leading this book project.

As I was gathering the stories of these women leaders, I was deeply touched by their faith, love and courage. We have many dedicated women who follow God's vision of reaching out to hurting people with the message of God's love and healing power. The world needs to hear how their faith has given them courage to overcome adversities and arise to help others. Their willingness to write their stories for future leaders made this book possible. I thank them for their dedication to helping future generations. May God bless and inspire whoever reads this book to know that there are many women who are the shining light in the darkness and who respond to their call to serve God and people.

Yong Hui V. McDonald

"BUT THOSE WHO HOPE IN THE LORD WILL RENEW THEIR STRENGTH."

(Isaiah 40:31A)

Women Who Lead

"THE PEOPLE LIVING IN DARKNESS HAVE SEEN A GREAT LIGHT." (Matthew 4:16A)

"But who would have thought that getting a Bible into the hands of the Ayoré people in their very own language would start with a little girl invited to a neighborhood Bible club. I never would have dreamed it."

— Maxine Morarie

Maxine Morarie

❧ 1 ❧

"Following My Heart"

By Maxine Morarie

By the time I was born –the 11th child in my family –
my folks had run out of names, so they gave the job
to my sisters. That's how I became Maxine Evon
Bailey. With a father who loved to entertain us, six
big brothers to tease me and four big sisters to spoil
me, it all made for a very happy childhood.

My Christian adventure began in the sixth grade
when I was invited to attend a neighborhood Bible
club. Having no idea what to expect, I dragged my
friend Leona along too. Neither of us had ever heard
the Gospel before. We weren't really sure what Jesus

had to do with anything except Christmas, but Mrs. Abel brought Him to life for us with songs and a flannel graph board and figures. I don't know how many times we attended before we understood the Gospel, but I do remember how emotional it was for me to accept Jesus as my Savior. Mrs. Abel then guided us to a good church in our neighborhood and explained how important it was to attend faithfully, which we did.

That next year we became more and more grounded in our faith and wanted to be baptized. My mother gave me permission, but Leona's mother wouldn't let her. Mrs. Abel interceded and we ended up being baptized on the same night – with no parent to view it. We were just two scared little girls on our own.

At 16, I was really challenged when I saw a film of the five NTM missionaries who were killed by the Ayorés in eastern Bolivia and heard NTM missionaries speak. I began to read everything I could get my hands on about New Tribes Mission. What Paul Fleming wrote really spoke to my teenage heart: "No man is too old to serve the Lord, and no man is too young." At the end of my junior year of high school our youth pastor and his wife and a group of young people from our church decided to go to California to study missions with New Tribes. The others were older than I was, but I decided to send in my application anyway. I figured if New Tribes accepted me, I would drop out of high school and go along. I fully expected to be turned down. I wasn't – and this caused a slight problem since I hadn't consulted my parents. With all my older siblings grown and gone and just my parents and me at home, I had become quite independent, and this was one of the consequences. Knowing my dad wouldn't want me to go without finishing high school, I answered an ad for the American School of Correspondence Courses, hoping I could take my senior year that way and still go.

After walking home one evening from where I worked at a popcorn stand, I was surprised to find an unknown gentleman in a suit sitting in our living room with my parents. "What's this about you wanting to take a correspondence course, young lady?" My daddy didn't look very happy.

Fearing there would be words, the man quickly stood up with his briefcase and prepared to leave. "I can see that she is a bit young, Mr. Bailey, and probably wouldn't have the determination to finish a correspondence course, so I'll just be going," he said. "Now, you just wait a minute, sir. If any one has determination, Maxine does!" And before I knew it, Daddy and the unknown gentleman from the American School of Correspondence Courses were planning the classes I'd need to finish my senior year.

After the man had gone, Daddy asked me, "Now, why in the world do you want to take your 12th grade by correspondence?"

And that's when I told my parents about wanting to go with New Tribes Mission in the fall. My folks just looked at each other. I knew they were thinking, "Whatever in the world put such an idea into her head?" But they always taught us to follow our hearts. Well, my heart was full of becoming a missionary.

The other person I needed to tell my plans to was Howard Morarie. We had met at church, but now he went to college quite a distance away in Fort Collins. We had been dating for a year, and he wasn't a very happy camper when I told him.

"Don't be silly," he pleaded. "I know you want to graduate. Then you can come up to Fort Collins, and I'll pay your way through college with my GI bill.

We can think about maybe becoming missionaries later."

"Well, I guess we'll have to break up then if you don't approve," I told him. And we did.

Then just a week before our group was to leave to begin missionary training in Fouts Springs, California, I was surprised to see Howard waiting in the foyer as I walked out of church on Sunday.

"Guess what I did?" Howard asked, with a big smile on his face.

"What did you do?" I asked cautiously.

"I sent in my application, and I'm going with you!"

In a whirlwind, we started the training in October 1949, got married the following August, and left for Bolivia in January 1951. With only our high school Spanish and a little additional study after our arrival, we were ready to launch in San José.

Howard wore many hats right off the bat. He helped the new little church in town, made supply runs and did the wiring for the new Tambo boarding school for missionaries' children that was under construction at the foot of the Andes Mountains. That left me alone much of the time. Our first two children were born during this time. I experienced fear and loneliness and struggled to learn Spanish. I remember the first time our son Howie smiled. Alone in San José, I wanted to tell someone, so I ran to one of the ladies from church. It wasn't until I started to tell her about it that I realized I didn't even know the word for 'smile.' I still don't know if she ever understood what I was trying to pantomime.

We were asked to move into Tobité where the Ayorés were – the very tribal people who had killed the first five missionaries. When I saw all of them running up the hill to meet us, I remember thinking, "What have we let ourselves in for?"

One of the Ayoré ladies immediately grabbed Nancy, who was ten months old, and with a grimy finger, began exploring her mouth for teeth. Up to that point, I had boiled everything that went into Nancy's mouth.

So I prayed, "Lord, you'll just have to protect the children now."

While Howard was busy teaching the Ayorés skills they would need – how to farm, saw lumber, cut railroad ties, understand the concept of money, etc. – I was busy having babies (six in all), helping deliver Ayoré babies, homeschooling, helping with literacy classes, and teaching women's and children's classes. Most of all, little-by-little I was learning the linguistics of the Ayoré language. And then one day, I was asked to begin translation of the Ayoré New Testament. Me! A wife and mother. I would have the privilege of translating a Bible for the Ayoré people. I felt so blessed.

Ecarai was my very first translation helper. We became very close as we worked together over the years. With his help, we discovered a term for 'born of the Spirit.' The Ayoré term for 'born' is 'to fall.' Not at all productive for born again. Fall again?

So one day, after puzzling over it a long time, Ecarai said, "I know what it is! It is like being washed into another clan. You are changed completely and all the things of the new clan are now for you to partake of." So we will say, "God's Spirit will clan-wash you and you will be changed into God's countrymen."

After that, whenever he would write me letters, he would close them with, "Your fellow clan-washed one by the Holy Spirit, Ecarai."

The translation took 12 years to complete and another three years to do the revision and see the New Testament in one volume. By the time it was finished, we had been in Bolivia for 32 years and decided it was time to go home and get to know our grandchildren. That is one adventure I'm still on.

But who would have thought that getting a Bible into the hands of the Ayoré people in their very own language would start with a little girl invited to a neighborhood Bible club. I never would have dreamed it.

When the Ayoré New Testament was printed by NTM Publications, we flew back to Bolivia for presentations in four different Ayoré villages, including Tobité where we had worked for so many years. Next we flew into Paraguay. The Mennonite community in Filadelfia hosted the first presentation there.

The whole town, Mennonites and Ayorés, showed up. Among them was the wife of a Mennonite missionary who had been killed by Ayorés years earlier. She was presented with one of the copies. After the ceremony, the widow requested another copy on behalf of her mother-in-law. She asked me if I would write something in it, relayed to her by her mother-in law, who was planning to give it away as a gift.

I was happy to oblige. Her mother-in-law wanted the Ayoré message to say, "This New Testament is presented to the man who killed my son. I want him to know that I forgive him and that I hope he will read God's Word and come to know Him."

Having completed the Ayoré New Testament, I began working on the Old Testament. With frequent trips to Paraguay, I was eventually able to translate 16 books of the Old Testament. When not working on the Ayoré translations, I was able to help translation projects get started in Mexico and also began training translators and checking translation in several Latin American countries.

In collaboration with others, an Ayoré/English dictionary was produced – a seven year project. Since that time I have translated that dictionary into Spanish/Ayoré, and that edition is now in print and in circulation in Bolivia and Paraguay.

When I look back over 64 years of missionary work, several people stand out as role models and mentors. Of course, I'll always be so glad that Mrs. Abel organized the Bible Club for grade schoolers in her neighborhood. Pastor Sherman Miller's heart for the Lord rubbed off on all of us young people in his church. He taught with large charts on major doctrinal themes and prophecy. He gave the Gospel with every teaching and led many, many people to the Lord. It almost felt as though we had already had Bible School because he took such pains to disciple us. Paul Fleming, founder of NTM, had a deep commitment to reach tribal people, no matter how small the tribe.

As a missionary he noticed that most mission work was done in the major languages of the world, and few missionaries learned tribal languages or translated Scripture for small tribes like the Ayoré. "If your sister was a tribal person," he would say, "and she lived in a small unknown tribe, you wouldn't think it wasted time and effort to break down her language and translate God's Word for her, when the only other alternative was eternity in Hell!"

Jean Dye Johnson, whose husband Bob had been killed by the Ayoré was my mentor, and it was she who encouraged me in my earliest efforts in linguistics and translation. But it was Wayne Gill who impacted my life the most. He was assigned to train me as a translator. He did all of the checking of my work and gave the approval for publication.

His life, his love of the Lord, and his dedication were things I found myself wanting to emulate! Before the Lord took him home, he had done the linguistic break down of two tribal groups and left them with New Testaments, hymn books, and study materials!

I am so very grateful that the Lord continues to open doors for me to serve Him, and my desire is to live in such a way as to draw many to the Lord as long as the Lord gives me life!

Author Bio

Maxine Morarie is a retired missionary who is still associated with New Tribes Mission in Sanford, Florida. She and her husband Howard, now deceased, served in Bolivia for 32 years. During much of that time, they worked with the Ayoré, an indigenous people who were originally hidden in the Green Hell Jungles of eastern Bolivia.

This tribe killed the first five New Tribes Missionary men who penetrated the jungle to search for them. Maxine and Howard were among the early missionaries who went in to work with this tribe. Maxine's main contributions were in the linguistic and translation areas, while Howard's were in the socio-economic development of the Ayoré. A hunter/gatherer society, the Ayoré had never heard of money or working for money.

Both Howard and Maxine preached and taught the word orally, and eventually a church grew out of their endeavors. Maxine has published a completed New Testament in that language, and a number of books of the Old Testament, a pedagogical grammar, dictionaries and many Bible Story/Bible Study books. After leaving Bolivia, the Moraries traveled to many countries where they taught translation and literacy skills to new missionaries in both English and

Spanish. The course materials for these were also published and used in the country of Colombia.

Currently, Maxine is engaged in developing resource materials for the Ayoré which she hopes will be available online in the near future, along with recorded Scripture broadcasts. She speaks in churches, colleges, women's retreats, and participates in jail ministries. She can be reached via email at maxine_morarie@ntm.org or by phone at 303-254-5561.

"TAKE AND EAT; THIS IS MY BODY."

(Matthew 26:26B)

"My life's purpose is to love God and to express that love by service to my fellow man through my work, my words, and my actions. Pick the area of life that arouses the most passionate response in you, and work in that area. You will become a leader."

— Laura Nokes Lang

Laura Nokes Lang

❧ 2 ❧

"Everything Is a Learning Experience"

By Laura Nokes Lang

I was named for my grandmother, and I took a lot of pride in that even though I had nothing to do with it, except I got born and named by my mother. My grandmother was a fantastic woman. She carried herself with dignity, and she did whatever it took to keep herself together after my grandfather died suddenly.

She lied about her age so she could get a job working in the New York City school system as a cafeteria lady, she took boarders into her home, she lived very frugally, and she invested wisely. She went to church every Sunday morning, and she kept herself fit physically. She was intensely loyal to her family.

We could do no wrong, and we didn't want to because if we came close, she was a strict disciplinarian. She had only an eighth grade education. I was 21 when she died, and I cried for days. Although she didn't have widespread influence in her community, she was definitely the matriarch of her family.

My mother and father were the super influences in my life. They used to rage at each other about everything, they drank way too much, and my father was gone for weeks and months at a time on business trips. My mother said that she realized that I was too stubborn to reach with physical punishment, so I say she set out to brainwash me.

Everything was turned into opportunities for her to tell me how young ladies should conduct themselves, how they should dress, how they should sit, how they should stand, how they should eat, how they should keep their home, how they should care for things, how they should conduct themselves, how they should speak, and whatever else happens in life. She said I should marry a college man, and then I would never have to worry. She did not allow me to work, and I could never do anything right enough to please her.

My father was a successful business executive, though he and my mother were only high school graduates. He was very angry most of the time I was growing up, so I was glad when he was gone away. As I matured, I realized that he was like two different people: mister wonderful mentor, highly honorable, charming, determined, brilliant thinker businessman and angry, drunk, mean-mouthed, physically abusive family man.

My brother was three years older than I, and he hated me from the moment I was born. He told me so after we were all grown up and I asked him what I had done to make him so mean to me. I couldn't do anything to change having been born into his family, so I just accepted that he would always hate me, and I had nothing more to do with him. He was a gutter-bum alcoholic from his late twenties until his late forties when he finally got sober in AA and stayed that way until he died at 56 from lung cancer.

He beat the alcohol, but not the cigarettes that were constantly hanging out of his mouth. He was a natural leader, though. People were just charmed by him somehow, and he had all kinds of success in politics and business until the alcohol took over his life. If I could figure out why people were so attracted to him, I would get some of that for me.

Like the good girl I was trying to be, I married a college man as soon as I graduated from college. My husband turned out to be a lot like my father, just not quite so successful in business. We had two children. I attended a mothers-of-preschoolers class while my children attended preschool classes. There I discovered that I had a knack for giving interesting speeches.

There was a commotion in my neighborhood about a proposed housing development on some nearby vacant land. I'm not sure how it happened, but I became a leader of the referendum petition drive to stop the development. It failed because the developer threatened to personally sue the two other sponsors of the petition.

They chickened out. I could not convince them to have the courage to exercise their right to petition. Life went on, and I can't say I accomplished anything remarkable. I had some difficult lessons in learning about leadership. You have to have a thick skin, that's for sure. I was the leader of one of the women's circles at my church. One of the ladies took exception to my leadership style which was to ask for participation from the ladies in the circle.

If no one wanted to do a project, then I would just submit our lack of interest to the powers that were instead of doing what past leaders had done which was to do the work for the whole circle. This woman called me on the phone and was very rude in what she had to say to me. I called the minister at the church to referee the situation, and he was willing to do that, so then she said more hateful things about me to him in my presence and stomped out of his office. He said something about her being a deeply troubled woman and not to take her seriously.

Life went on. I tried to start a home-based business but had little success with it. I didn't have any passion for it although I totally love the concepts and products that I was supposed to promote. No passion equated to no performance equated to no success.

I joined a group of small business owners and professional sales people to try to learn more about developing my business, and still did nothing with it. What I did discover is that I really enjoyed developing programs and planning parties for the club. I stayed active in that role in that club for many years, gave hours and hours of time and piles of energy to it, and I was given many awards by the club for my good work.

I really enjoyed bringing in trainers and speakers to help these people with their professional development, but I still did very little with my own business. Now that I am past retirement age, I may do something with it.

Life keeps happening while we are making other plans. My son committed suicide at the age of 20. My heart broke, and it still isn't healed after all these years. He was the joy of my life – full of mischief, full of fun, full of enthusiasm for life. He was everything I always wanted to be but never quite was.

I became obsessed with understanding why he killed himself. After months of research, interviews, and consideration of everything I could learn, I came to believe that he took his own life because he was in an alcohol induced psychotic state in which he decided he was not good enough to live.

I thought that his life and death were meaningless unless I used what he had done and what I had learned to teach people about the possible consequences of alcohol abuse. I started going to high schools, middle schools, colleges, and civic groups to give speeches about what happened to Keith. I realized that there was only one of me, and I could not possibly reach everyone who would benefit from hearing what I had to say. I founded KGN Corporation, a Colorado non-profit organization with a 501 (c) 3 designation from the IRS, in the hope that people would donate money to support my efforts.

I decided to develop a video presentation that could reach many more students than would be able to hear me personally. It is still in national distribution, though it is not a best seller. I continued giving speeches as before.

At the twentieth anniversary of Keith's suicide, I decided to do another video for the benefit of suicide survivors. Keith's sister and several of his friends were willing to be interviewed for this video, and now it is in national distribution, as well. The point is to try to help new survivors realize that they will get through the deep grief, it doesn't go on for the rest of your life, and shows different ways that people have dealt with their grief. It is not a best seller, either.

While all of that was happening, my husband and I divorced. He remarried shortly, and a couple of years later, I married a wonderful guy. He died after four and a half years from cancer, but they were very meaningful years for me. My daughter said at his memorial service that, "He was the best thing that every happened to my mom in her life – even better than me and my brother."

Norman taught me about things from the trivial to the deeply meaningful. He had a brilliant intellect and was a Christian in his soul. I think the most important lessons for me were that I am lovable and acceptable, just as I am. Learning this allowed me to be more accepting of others as they are, and this has changed many relationships in my life.

About eight years ago, I had the opportunity to present my little speech to inmates at Adams County Detention Facility in Brighton, Colorado. The inmates were very nice to me, and I think some of them made some healthy decisions about how they would live their lives when they got out of jail. That was gratifying.

The Chaplain was working on some stories that prisoners had written about their sense of God being with them while they were incarcerated. They were wonderful stories that I had a chance to read between speeches. The Chaplain asked me whether I would help her with the book of these stories she was developing for use with the inmates. I was honored to be asked, and I started editing some of the stories.

Life went on. Eventually, the need for a formal organization became evident. I helped prepare the documents necessary for incorporation in Colorado and for application for Transformation Project Prison Ministry (TPPM) to get a 501 (c) 3 designation from the IRS, based on my experience with KGN. I tried to be supportive of the work in every way I could because I really believed in the good that was coming from the books for everyone involved: the writers, editors, publishers, shippers, and the final readers.

Many years ago, I was curious to learn what on earth was going on politically as President Nixon was in deep trouble and in fact resigned. I went to a precinct caucus and was elected to be precinct committeewoman. I didn't even know what that was. I learned that it was work and that I received very little support from people in my area, mainly because I was a Republican and almost everyone around was a Democrat.

I was re-elected to the position one time, but then there was turmoil in the party, the few Republicans in the area loaded the caucus with people who shared their particular view, knocked me out of my slot and were never heard from again. Now, that's not fair.

If you put yourself in a leadership position, then you need to do the work of leadership. I joined the Republican Trumpeteers of Adams County, now known as Adams County Republican Women/ Trumpeteers. Someone said that they would appreciate my being the corresponding secretary. I wasn't sure what that was, but I took the job because no one else was excited about doing the work.

Yes. The job was work. I felt I was helping my political cause in a way that I could. We are each given different talents and abilities, and I used mine as well as I could for the good of the club. We haven't caused anyone to win an election, but we give support as we are able.

Behind most of my adult life and the development I have had emotionally and spiritually is a Twelve Step recovery group. There I learned principles for living that work when I work them. They involve such things as turning my will and my life over to the care of God, as I understand God; realizing that I cannot control other people, places, or things, that I am darned lucky if I can control myself; knowing that God will give me the strength to do the things that are in His will for me to do; doing the highest and best good that I can; giving people a hand up will yield better results than giving people a handout.

I seem to be a leader in this group, although we have no designated leaders. I think people listen to me there because they have to and because I have been in the program for over 30 years and longevity counts for something.

If I had it to do all over again, I would be born into a happy family and my whole life would be different. If I had it to do all over again, I would have done well in school, gone to an Ivy League university and become a great lawyer – or something – and my whole life would be different. If I had it to do all over again, I would have stayed single and not had any kids. My life would be so different now. If I had it to do all over again, I would have found some volunteers with really great marketing skills to come and help me with my KGN work.

The information I want to share could save many lives, and it helps no one locked in a video case. If I had it to do all over again, I would have gotten into a Twelve Step program a lot sooner because it gave me tools to live life, to love God, and loving God, to love myself, and loving myself, to love others. I could have been doing that all along instead of going through so much misery alone.

My statement of my life's purpose pretty well sums up what I think every leader needs: "My life's purpose is to love God and to express that love by service to my fellow man through my work, my words, and my actions." Pick the area of life that arouses the most passionate response in you, and work in that area. You will become a leader.

Author Bio

Laura Nokes Lang is the Director of KGN Corporation, a Colorado non-profit organization with a 501 (c) 3 designation from the IRS. KGN is dedicated to the prevention of alcohol abuse and suicide through education. Ms. Nokes Lang founded KGN following the death of her son in 1991, and since that time has presented programs in high schools, middle schools, churches, and civic groups all over the state of Colorado and in Nebraska. She produced two videos now in national distribution: "Let It Not Be In Vain," and "Grief after a Suicide – a 20-Year Perspective."

Ms. Nokes Lang has served in leadership positions in several non-profit organizations and her church. She currently resides in Westminster, Colorado, with her dog G.G. Being an optimist, Ms. Nokes Lang named her puppy G.G. which is an abbreviation for "Good Girl."

"YOU ARE THE LIGHT OF THE WORLD."

(Matthew 5:14A)

"We serve a BIG God, so make sure you dream BIG. Don't be afraid, don't listen to the naysayers, don't get discouraged and most of all don't let ANYONE talk you out of your vision and your dream. With God all things are possible."
— Angela McMahan

Angela McMahan

❧ 3 ❧

"Arising Dreams"

By Angela McMahan

It didn't happen at all how I thought it would. I thought I would quit my nice government job, raise and apply for lots of money, build a beautiful facility, and THEN the women I wanted to serve would come. That's not at all how it happened.

I was going through a horrible divorce from the man who abused me, I was upside down on my mortgage and three months behind in the payments, and I was eating beans and rice for every meal because I didn't qualify for any assistance programs. I was emotionally broken and could barely take care of myself, yet everywhere I went I started running into women just like me.

I'd be in the ladies room and a woman would tell me her husband beat her last night. I would be standing in line at motor vehicle and see the black eye and bruises of the woman in front of me. I signed up to volunteer with a local battered women's shelter where in training they talked about "those girls" as if there was some hierarchy between them and those that where staying with them at the shelter.

I was at a monthly Bible study when a young girl kept coming and telling stories of extreme emotional abuse that was happening to her, and was continually told by the leaders to "go home and pray about it – try to make his favorite meal and he will stop." Yet week after week her situation continued to get worse and worse. I guess you could say that God was trying to get my attention. And eventually I just could not turn a blind eye to what I was seeing.

I guess I should take you back and start from the beginning. A little over ten years ago, I woke up face down in a pool of my own blood. It was an early Sunday morning. It was about 4:00 AM. I was beaten, battered and bruised. I was left for dead. I was left on cold, hard cement in my garage by the one person who was supposed to love me, care for me "until death do us part."

I have no idea of how long I lay there. I was not sure what was happening when I woke up. The scene around me looked more like a horror scene. There was a broken coffee table, items in disarray or turned over and my blood was everywhere.

I knew I was in trouble, and I knew that if something didn't drastically change in my life that I was going to die in this place. I struggled to my knees and I looked up and I cried out; "Lord, if anything I ever heard about you was true," and "If you are real, then I need your help!!!" I promised God. "If you will help me I will serve you the rest of my days, just PLEASE help me." "I don't want to live like this anymore!" "I don't want to die."

I was married in August of 2001. I never really aspired to wanting much more than to be a wife and mom. I dreamed about my wedding day my whole life. I thought this man was my soul mate. Up until that moment in my life, no man had ever lavished such gifts on me before or taken me to such exquisite restaurants. I was young, naïve and in love. I was finally getting the family I had always wanted and dreamed about.

No one ever marries thinking it will end in divorce, or abuse, or even worse, death. Oh sure, now looking back I see all the warning signs: domestic violence and assault charges in his past, the negativity when he spoke about women, his angry outburst in public when he didn't get his way, the way he seemed to talk to me at times as if I was nothing, nobody or completely worthless and the times that he just seemed to "show up" wherever I was.

From the moment I married him my whole world became about pleasing him. Weeks after my wedding day, I would lay awake at night and wonder, who was this person that I had married? Where had that wonderful, sweet, charming and loving man that I knew gone? Who was this angry, jealous, possessive, controlling person that I now lived with day to day? Oh, I suppose if he had hit me on our first date I would have never seen him again; but the changes were subtle and slow over time, they didn't just happen overnight.

Every relationship that I had became difficult. It was my secret, and no one understood why I didn't call them back anymore; why I couldn't go out to dinner with my friends anymore; and why I didn't even see my mom for five years. Oh sure, he said it was okay for me to go, but there was always hell to pay when I returned home.

My work loved me and I shined there. I never wanted to be at home anymore, so I would go to work early and stay late, anything not to have to go home. But work only loved me when I was there. They soon tired of me calling in sick and the continual excuses and reasons why I wouldn't be in the office that day.

I had become to everyone else a person who didn't follow through, couldn't be counted on or depended upon. I lacked character and integrity. When I said "yes" or committed myself to an event, I really wanted to show up and my spouse "Said" he was supportive, yet why was it so hard to get out of the house: the fighting, the yelling, the accusations, the questioning, the insecurity the complete insanity.

I didn't think love was supposed to hurt or that someone who said they cared about you could hurt you so badly. My life had become a constant and continual fight. He was always mad and I was always to blame. If I had a bad day, he had a worse day. So, I stuffed down my pain and told myself that I was FINE (Freaked out, Insecure, Neurotic and Emotional)!

My life became a pattern of dysfunction and destruction. He would abuse me and then I would abuse myself in one way, shape or form. Friday nights became all about the "party." Oh sure, in the beginning I was very liberal minded about drugs and alcohol. We were just social drinkers and druggers, after all. We would "dabble" in it if it was around. However, it was around every weekend, and a casual night out with friends quickly became an eight-ball a week habit. Towards the end, no one had to force me to get high.

Fridays became my worst day of the week. I would be sick and throwing up in the bathroom at work because of the fear and thoughts of having to go home for the weekend. Would I live to see Monday morning? I would hit the door of my house on Friday evenings and drink and drug as fast as I could so that I just wouldn't have to remember the things that would be said and done to me that weekend, all in the name of love.

My life had become a toxic pattern where he abused me, I numbed and tuned out with drugs and alcohol, and then the pain would build up and I would ultimately take razor blades and cut myself. When his abuse stopped mine began.

I knew my life was becoming unmanageable and spiraling out of control. I knew I needed help. I started to see a therapist for the "cutting." She told me I was being abused at home.

I said that's impossible; "I have a psychology degree and I'm a professional business woman who goes to work every day. I just think I am under too much stress and don't understand why I am cutting. Besides, my husband hasn't hit me."

She looked at me and said, "Sweetie, he doesn't have to hit you. Look at you; he's got you beating yourself up!"

And truthfully, a better statement would have been; "He hadn't hit me yet!" I didn't know that pushing, shoving, hovering, blocking my exits, holding me down on the bed, sitting on me and bear hugs that I couldn't break free from are all forms of physical violence. However, all of this was locked behind the door of a beautiful ranch home in the suburbs. This was my secret! No one knew what was happening to me! And I didn't know how to tell them, how to ask for help. After all, wasn't fighting part of any marriage?

But that day in my garage, it all changed. That day a light bulb went off in my head, and I knew that I had to leave this life or I was going to die. If he didn't hurt me, then I was going to overdose on the drugs and alcohol, and if the drugs and alcohol didn't hurt me then I was going to eventually cut too deep. The truth is I never wanted to die, and I really didn't want to get divorced. I said for "better or worse" and I meant it – I just wanted the PAIN to stop!

Eventually, he was removed from the house and we separated and started divorce proceedings. I was so happy to be free, I had forgotten all about the promise I had made about serving God the rest of my days. Now, I was calling all my girlfriends and family members I hadn't seen in the past five years and we were "going to the club." It's difficult to explain even today, but I would come home drunk, yet I had this constant "nagging" feeling like I needed to go back to church.

My partying lasted only three weeks before I walked back into my local church. The minute I walked in, an usher handed me a choir audition flyer. I looked up, laughed and said, "NO WAY!!!" Then throughout the service, my Bishop was talking about serving in your local church and about how a big church becomes a small church once you get involved. The only singing I had ever done was maybe some karaoke here and there, yet after service I found myself standing in line outside the choir room doors.

I never forgot the audition form, it asked questions like: Are you a member of this church? "Ahhh, No!" Do you tithe? "No, again!" Do you smoke? "Yes!" Do you drink? "Sometimes!" I knew enough not to lie in church, but I thought to myself, forget about my singing ability, they are never going to let me into this choir based on my morality issues. Yet they must have seen something in me that I could not, because two days later they called and congratulated me that I was now a member of the Heritage Christian Center

Mass Choir (now known as The Potter's House
Church of Denver Mass Choir).

Once I got involved in the choir, they asked me to
sing with their praise team and that led me to being
asked by a good friend to sing with the Celebrate
Recovery Praise Team. There was just one catch;
I had to take a class called "Life Hurts God Heals."
To say I was less than thrilled is an understatement.
I was downright mad. All I could think is Lord this is
so NOT FAIR. I was the one abused, I was the one
who had to get an attorney, I was the one who even
had to pack up his belongings, and now I have to take
a recovery class, too.

I remember my first day, I told my Pastor (who
now is a very good friend of mine); "Look, I have
TWO psych degrees, I am just here to see how you
Christian folk do this counseling thing!!!" He said
well, okay, then come right in and have a seat. By the
time I attended the second class, I knew I needed to
be there. Yes, I had survived the abuse but I was
forever changed (both good and bad), by the events
that took place while living in that situation. I had
picked up some pretty nasty habits and survival skills
along the way that while in an abusive marriage
helped me to survive, but sadly were hurting me in the
real world.

Almost every relationship I had now was struggling. I was struggling with any type of authority figure, like my parents and my boss. I had such a chip on my shoulder because "No one was ever going to hurt me again!" and "No one is going to tell me what to do!" The first time I tried to date, I was displaying almost stalker behavior. I was trying to control everything and everyone so that I wouldn't get hurt again, or worse, make the same mistakes. Yet the truth is I was only continuing to hurt myself.

That class forever changed my life. Not only did it completely remove the hurt and pain of my abusive marriage, but it even dealt with some unresolved childhood issues, too. For the first time in my life, I could look myself in the mirror and be proud of the person I was. I started to dream again and ask myself questions like; "What could I really do and be in my life if no one was telling me who and what I was?" "What was my purpose, and why was I created?"

I came up with a wonderful idea and plan: the church should start a faith based domestic violence shelter. I put together a beautiful presentation, took it to the counseling department, and asked for a meeting with Bishop.

They too agreed it was a fantastic idea, so they looked at me and said; "So you will be the Director?" I said, "Oh no" I have a full time day job – I couldn't possible do that! They then informed me, that the church was averaging about 1-5 calls per day from women in crisis, and when could they start referring? After that conversation, I started doing some research and looking into what it would take to start a shelter in my area. In November of 2007 Arising Hope was incorporated.

The woman I mentioned earlier who was attending Bible study with me became my first client. I just started bringing women, children and pets home with me. Before I knew it I had five women, five kids, three dogs and two cats all staying with me in my little three bedroom house. And so began Arising Hope.

Arising Hope is committed to offering hope and healing to victims of domestic violence by providing a safe place of love and empowerment. Our goals are: to give safe emergency housing and shelter to women, their children and their domestic pets victimized by domestic violence; to provide biblically-based counseling and classes which offer hope and healing for victims of abuse; to educate the community to the serious effects of domestic violence; to empower women with life-skills, job and financial counseling and training; and to end future violence by working with the public and local community.

I am often asked, "How do you start a non-profit?" I will be honest with you, it hasn't been easy, and there are many challenging days when I want to quit. Yet, God is so faithful, and He gives me just what I need at just the right time to work another day.

My suggestions are always the same. Find your nearest local business office through the city or county where you live or want to start the business. Contact them and tell them your plans to start a non-profit business. They will send you a business packet that has all of the information you need to get started. Typically, first steps are: 1. Incorporate with the state you live in, 2. Get your Federal Employer Identification Number and apply for a 501(c) 3 designation with the IRS. 4. Then get a state sales tax exemption certificate. 5. Get a website.

I never dreamed my life could be so awesome, amazing, fantastic and happy. I am so grateful to my God for keeping me to the promise I made Him that day not so long ago, for teaching me that it's not about religion, it's about relationship. I could never have imagined that I would be a successful business women and leader, that President and CEO would follow after my name.

He is the God of second, third and fourth chances; as many as we need to get it right. He is no respecter of persons, so what He has done for me, He can and will do for you.

Oh sure, I still have trials and tribulations, but my worst day now doesn't even come close to comparing to my best day then. I no longer have a desire to smoke, drink, drug or party. Truth is, I am having such a great life I don't want to "tune out" and miss a moment of it! I also have come to meet and befriend some of the most loving and beautiful people on the planet.

We serve a BIG God, so make sure you dream BIG. Don't be afraid, don't listen to the naysayers, don't get discouraged, and most of all, don't let ANYONE talk you out of your vision and your dream. With God all things are possible.

Author Bio

Angela McMahan is the President and CEO of Arising Hope International, a Christ-Centered domestic violence shelter in Denver, Colorado. She started the shelter in her home in November of 2007. Arising Hope is the only faith based shelter in Colorado and provides residential treatment to women, their children and their pets who are victims of domestic violence.

The shelter has received recognition from the American Humane Association as the first PAWS shelter in Colorado and is currently recognized in the National SAF-T (Shelter Animals and Families Together) Program. Arising Hope has also received awards for their efforts to be green and keep clothing and textiles out of landfills.

Angela is an accomplished public speaker, co-author, teacher and facilitator of the Road to Freedom and Road to Healing programs taught weekly at the shelter and local churches throughout the Denver metropolitan area. Currently the curriculum is taught every Monday evening at 6 PM at the Potter's House of Denver, 9495 E Florida Ave, Denver, Colorado 80247 in room 220 and every Wednesday and Thursday at the Adams County Detention Facility in Brighton, Colorado.

She currently resides in Thornton, Colorado with her two dogs; Grace and Lexi and her two cats; Izzy and Hannah.

"LET YOUR LIGHT SHINE BEFORE MEN,
THAT THEY MAY SEE YOUR GOOD DEEDS
AND PRAISE YOUR FATHER IN HEAVEN."
(Matthew 5:16B)

"Real leadership, I think, comes when you know and love yourself. Because when you know who you are and love yourself, you can love others as well. Sound relationship, sincerity, and a strong sense of commitment rather than one's ability are more desirable qualities of successful leaders... God gave each of us different talents. When we use our God-given talents for His work, He empowers us as leaders."

— Sung Hea Rhim

Sung Hea Rhim

❧ **4** ❧

"Making a Difference"

By Sung Hea Rhim
Translated by Lija Kim

"There are three kinds of people in the world: those who are necessary for this world, those who aren't, and those whose presence doesn't matter. I hope all of you belong to the first category."

This remark by my high school teacher stayed with me throughout my life. I wanted to live my life as somebody who could make a positive difference in this world.

I was born 40 days after the Korean War broke out on June 25, 1950, as the youngest child in the family with two other siblings. I was a happy baby, much loved by my parents, but the Korean War brought tragic changes to my life. My father was kidnapped by North Koreans, and my mother became a young widow with three small children. My mother was a well-educated woman with financial security. Instead of raising her children as other Korean mothers would do under a similar situation, she entrusted us to my grandparents' care and went on to live her own life.

Since my grandfather was a medical doctor, I was well-provided for materially. But I missed my parents' presence and their love very much. I still remember those days, feeling left out when other classmates' parents came to discuss their student's progress report during my elementary school years.

I was a bright student in elementary school so I was accepted to the very competitive Ewha Junior High, Ewha High School and went on to Ewha Womans University. They were all founded by a Methodist missionary, Mary Scranton. Though Ewha was a Christian school, I was not a Christian while I was in school.

Even after graduation from the university I never felt the need for religious belief of any kind. As my marriage approached, my then parents-in-law-to-be suggested to me that I attend church and be baptized someday. They gave me a Bible as one of my engagement gifts. My grandfather saw the present and told me I got the best gift. That's how I started to attend church and was baptized.

When I went to church for the first time after my arrival in the United States, I was asked to teach at Sunday school. I hesitated because I never attended Sunday school as a child. People at the church knew that I was a kindergarten teacher, and they told me being a Sunday school teacher is not that different from being a kindergarten teacher.

By nature, saying "no" to people was not easy for me so I accepted the challenge. Out of a strong sense of responsibility I studied the Bible very diligently and taught the children. Ever since then I have been serving the Lord in many positions.

In November, 2003, there was a turning point in my life. It was becoming an officer in United Methodist Women where I am serving with passion even now.

A life-changing event happened to me when a Korean sister in Christ asked me to work as an officer of the New York Conference UMW Korean Network. Until then my church involvement was limited only to the local unit. At first I insisted I had been serving the church in every conceivable way and position and there was nothing more I could do. But the Lord sent me somebody who was more stubborn than I. It was Myung Rae Lee who has passion for the mission for women, children and youth. She persuaded me to attend the Korean Network meeting. Come to think of it even now, it is not easily comprehensible that I rode a train *alone* from New Jersey where I was living at that time to Long Island to attend this meeting.

I never met Myung Rae before and I didn't even know those people who were supposed to be there. It was a miracle that I went to a place I had never been before to be with people I never met. By nature I never go anyplace *alone*. There is no coincidence in life. There I met Reverend Hea Sun Kim who happened to have given a moving sermon at my church on the previous Mother's Day.

I invited Reverend Hea Sun Kim again as the speaker for our dedication service on May 12th, 1996, when I became our local unit UMW president. After the service, in my mind I thought it would be good to work for UMW with Reverend Kim later in my life. Seven years later I met Reverend Kim again. In 1993 she started a leadership training and spiritual growth study for Korean women who immigrated to America.

That's how I became involved with United Methodist Women as one of its members. My involvement with UMW brought a rapid change in my life.

When I first read the UMW purpose, the phrase, "to experience freedom as whole persons through Jesus Christ," posed a big challenge to me. As I mentioned in the beginning, I grew up without my parents and always craved their love. In prayer one day, I heard the Lord's voice, "Sung Hea, do you know how much I love you?"

When I realized God took me as His child and loved me so much that He sent His only son, Jesus, to give me eternal life, I felt so blessed, and I thought whining about lack of my parents' love looked selfish. And I realized that I was a woman who experienced freedom as a whole person through Jesus Christ. I said to myself from now on I should free myself from the yoke of the past and live like God's child and as a disciple of Jesus.

I also learned the history of the United Methodist Women. In 1884, Lucinda Brown Baldwin, a Methodist woman from Ravenna, Ohio, donated $88 to help women of Chosun (Korea) who were living in the dark without knowing the good news of the gospel. Not many people at that time knew there was

a country called Chosun. One woman's love for
Christ was able to inspire the missionary, Mary
Scranton, to bring a miracle in Korea through a long
journey of dedication and sacrifice. I listened to their
selfless and beautiful stories in tears. God was
gracious and loving even to me who was living like a
self-satisfied frog in a little pond.

Several months after I started to work as a UMW
officer, I had an opportunity to go to United
Methodist Committee on Relief Sager-Brown Depot
in Louisiana for mission training. There I saw a poster
on the wall that said, "What kind of change did you
make in another person's life?" And I asked myself,
"Have I been living my life as a person who is a
positive influence on other people? What have I done
for my neighbors?"

During an early prayer service a few years back,
the verse from chapter 13 of 1 Corinthians, "love is
not self-seeking...," came to my mind. Up until then
I knew that I prayed only for my family's blessings.
I realized why God touched my heart with this
particular verse. At the closing worship service at
UMCOR I made up my mind to serve the Lord and
His people, singing the hymn with tears in my eyes,
"Here I am Lord, Is it I, Lord? I have heard you

calling in the night. I will go Lord if you lead me. I will hold your people in my heart." I made a promise to the Lord to follow Him as his disciple for transformation of the world and I have been trying my best ever since then not to disappoint Him.

I just obeyed and followed the path He prepared for me. During the last 10 years, I ran that path very fast.

As a UMW officer I learned many things through leadership training, matured spiritually through retreats, and realized who my neighbors were. The UMW trainings focus on spiritual growth, participation in social justice, leadership development, and concepts of mission. Through these trainings, I was able to examine myself deeply and opened my eyes to things I never realized existed in this world, such as human trafficking, immigration issues, domestic violence, gender inequality, and racial discrimination.

I also met many Christian sisters who knew that the Bible taught them how to live but didn't know how to apply those teachings to their own lives. So I developed programs for United Methodist Women, resources for training and retreats, and leadership development programs, so my sisters in faith could use these tools for their own betterment.

Since 2003 I have been working as an officer and adviser of United Methodist Women, the president of the National Network of Korean UMW, president of New York Conference UMW Korean Network, and a member of the board of directors of Kor-Sage Leadership Center.

I also led various workshops at leadership training events. Whenever I am asked to give a speech at Young Women's Leadership Training events, I tell them they are fortunate and blessed to be able to get leadership training at a young age when many people including myself started training much later in their lives. I also tell them that I hope they experience freedom as whole persons through Jesus Christ and live a life of a leader who can bring positive change to this world.

Nowadays you can read up on leadership qualities and famous leaders through the internet and other media. It is easy to get information on the subject and learn. What kind of a leader do I want to be? What leadership qualities do I possess? If you really want, you can find all of these very easily. And depending on the kind of organization, different leadership styles will be needed. Real leadership, I think, comes when you know and love yourself. Because when you know who you are and love yourself, you can love others as well. Sound relationship, sincerity, and a strong sense of commitment rather than one's ability are more desirable qualities of successful leaders.

Many people tend to compare themselves with others and think they cannot be good leaders. They tend to think leaders have to be born with special leadership qualities. God gave each of us different talents. When we use our God-given talents for His work, He empowers us as leaders.

Philippians 4:13, says, "I can do everything through him who gives me strength." I hope, you trust in the Lord and answer "yes," with gratitude, to His calling.

I majored in education at college and am working as a public school teacher now. Every day as I teach my students I realize the importance of education through my personal experience. I learned many things through UMW training and opened my eyes to many different areas that I never thought existed.

My positive attitude to learn new things with sincerity brought me this far. I will continue to work hard to be the leader who is a positive influence to the world. I know we can learn, grow, and put our plans into action through active participation together for the advancement of women. I am thankful to God that He had a plan for my life, guided me and let me participate in His ministries. As He let me see and hear by sending the Holy Spirit to me, I just pray now that I live my life as a loyal stewardess who obeys His calling to build His kingdom in this world for His people.

Lastly I want to share one of my favorite stories with you. The Starfish Story: one step towards changing the world.

By Peter Straube

Early one morning, an old man was walking along the shore after a big storm had passed and found the vast beach littered with starfish as far as the eye could see, stretching in both directions. Off in the distance, the old man noticed a small boy approaching. As the boy walked, he paused every so often and as he grew closer, the man could see that he was occasionally bending down to pick up an object and throw it into the sea. The boy came closer still and the man called out, "Good morning! May I ask what it is that you are doing?" The

young boy paused, looked up, and replied "Throwing starfish into the ocean. The tide has washed them up onto the beach and they can't return to the sea by themselves," the youth replied. "When the sun gets high, they will die, unless I throw them back into the water." The old man replied, "But there must be tens of thousands of starfish on this beach. I'm afraid you won't really be able to make much of a difference." The boy bent down, picked up yet another starfish and threw it as far as he could into the ocean. Then he turned, smiled and said, "It made a difference to that one!"
"It made a difference to that one!"

Author Bio

Sung Hea Rhim is currently chair person of the National Network of Korean –American United Methodist women. She has served as a president of this organization for the last four years. She was a board member of Kor-Sage Leadership Center. She loves to develop programs for retreats and workshops for leadership training. She has led many workshops, retreat and leadership trainings in the USA.

She was a member of The United Methodist Council on Korean-American Ministries. She joined United Methodist Women in 2005 and fell in love with the purpose of UMW. Ever since, she has participated with passion, dedication and joy.

She has been a member of the Korean Methodist Church and Institute in New York since 1975 and served as a chair person in many different ministries. She is a Lay Servant. She also was an officer in the New York Conference of United Methodist Women.

She has been an educator for more than 30 years and taught autistic, learning disability and emotionally disturbed children in public school for the last 16 years. She received her bachelor's degree in Early Childhood Education at Ewha Womans University in Seoul Korea.

"The abuse and loss of control I experienced in my childhood and in my marriage taught me the submission and detachment that I would understand as an adult and would use to focus on loving God and detaching from worldly distractions. My pain taught me to have compassion for others who were struggling."
– Lynette McClain

Lynette McClain

✺ 5 ✺

"Tough Lessons"

By Lynette McClain

"Hardships often prepare ordinary people for an extraordinary destiny..."

C.S. Lewis

I was born in 1950. The culture in those days was much different than it is now. Many women born in my era can relate to my relationship with my mother. My mother had hopes and dreams for her life. She was creative, smart, talented, and fun loving. She loved people and always had a fascinating story to tell. She was energetic and curious and motherhood was not on her top 10 list of things to accomplish as a young woman of 19. When she became a mother, she sacrificed all of her hopes and dreams and had to grow up very quickly. Luckily, she idolized her boyfriend, my dad, so she focused her life on supporting his achievements and was instrumental in making his dreams become a reality. The result of this type of sacrifice is a sort of empty satisfaction. Especially when the sacrifice doesn't end well.

After twisting and turning to force things to happen, my father saw a person who had just twisted herself into a quite an unappetizing pretzel. It didn't help either that my mother frequently showed her resentments with irrational behaviors, misplaced rage, and blame. She felt like a victim and she acted like it, at every opportunity.

Still, my parents were committed to staying together for the children and making an effort to have as normal a family life as they knew how to have. I believe they did the best they could to do the right thing, which was probably very difficult to do when their heart wasn't in it. I am grateful to them for the efforts they made.

When I was born, my parents were not prepared for parenthood. They were both young and just really liked sex! They had two abortions before I came along, but this time, my grandmother refused to arrange it and so they were forced to have me. They had an active social life and I'm sure a baby definitely put a crimp in their young lives. They were married 6 months before I was born, which was shameful in those days. My mom had to drop out of college. She has had dreams of becoming an interior decorator. They both did their best, but my brother and I just weren't top priority and we knew it from the very beginning. If we didn't remember, my mother was sure to remind us throughout our lives.

When I was 3 and my brother was 6 months old, my mother contracted polio. She was paralyzed from the neck down and was told she would never walk again. Everyday, my father worked with my mother to do stretching and strengthening exercises on her legs. After two years, she was able to walk again!

There was a polio epidemic during this time in the early 50's and polio was highly contagious, so my parents had a hard time finding childcare for my brother and me. My 80-year-old great grandmother was often the only one available so, at the early age of 3, I began assisting with the care of my baby brother. We ate a lot of Cracker Jacks and Cheetos and drank a lot of Tang!

My dad was raised Catholic and was sent away to

a high school for Catholic Christian Brothers between the ages of 14 and 15. He was taught to be submissive and felt he was being treated poorly by the priests, so he came back to Denver and joined the Navy at the age of 17 and earned his GED in the Navy. He was the eighth and youngest child in his family and was very close to his family, but his mother told him she never wanted to see him again after he married my mother, a Lutheran. We would sometimes visit our paternal grandparents on Christmas, but were treated as outsiders from the rest of the relatives.

My maternal grandparents were very close to our family. My grandfather had an 8th grade education and worked for Union Pacific Railroad, painting the stenciled letters on the sides of the cars. We stayed at their house about once a week when my parents went out and they both fussed over us. Those were some of my best memories.

My grand parents were very active in the Lutheran church. My parents attended the Lutheran church too and both taught Sunday School for a few years. I sang in the church choir as a teen-ager and was confirmed in the Lutheran Church. I remember wanting to marry a Lutheran minister from a very young age.

My mother loved to shop. She and my father liked

having nice things and enjoyed annual family vacations, but they both had a difficult time managing their money. Their credit cards were always maxed out and they struggled each month to make ends meet. They argued a lot, mostly about money. My mother had a hot temper and my dad never said too much, which made my mom even madder.

In addition to teaching, my dad always had 1 or 2 side jobs and was not around much. He was also active in the local volunteer fire department. From time to time, my mother worked part-time jobs. She was also very active in volunteer organizations like PTA, Girls Scouts, door-to-door political canvassing, police department volunteering, pet therapy in nursing homes, and sewing projects.

She loved to sew and made most of my clothes. I never really appreciated this as I had little say about the style, color, or fabrics. I suppose it could have been worse, because she was pretty talented in her creations and I never felt embarrassed to wear anything she made. (Luckily, I don't remember my toddler years and wearing the little dresses that matched hers!)

My mother was very critical of my appearance and selected all of my clothing and did my hair until

I was into my late teens. As a result, I still don't trust myself to pick out clothing.

In that same vein, my mother wanted me to be a specific type of person. I think she was mostly disappointed with who I was becoming. She wanted me to be something wonderful and I just never quite measured up. Perhaps she was living her life through me. I was entered in a beautiful baby contest at age 1 and I took ballet and tap dance lessons beginning at around age 4 and performed in many recitals. I took ballroom and square dancing at age 10-13. I was enrolled in charm school modeling classes at age 13. At age 8, I began Girl Scouts until age 14.

My parents would spank us to punish us. I seldom got spanked, but I remember several times, as young as age 6, I had to go to school with make-up on my face to hide bruises from one parent or the other hitting me in the face. I was a timid, shy, awkward girl. I can remember wondering why I couldn't just relax in my body, but I always felt uncomfortable in front of people. I felt as if there was something wrong with me, but I didn't know what that was. Later people would tell me that I seemed sort of sad and serious as a kid. I think I just felt unlovable.

My mother had mental health issues, which, to my

knowledge, have never been diagnosed or treated. The most memorable event took place when I was about 9 and my brother about 6. My parents thought they had a coupon for a reduced hotel rate in Las Vegas. We drove to Las Vegas for the weekend. As we packed to go back home, my dad went to pay the bill and realized that he had mistaken the coupon offering.

The desk clerk told him that the coupon was only for certain days of the week and we would have to pay full price for our room. When my mother found out, she hit the roof. She kept yelling at my dad to go back and talk to them and insist that they give him the rate promised on the coupon. My dad kept explaining that he had already done that and that they were not going to give him the reduced rate. My mom wanted my dad to make a big scene and he refused.

We loaded our things in the car and left. In the car, my mom continued yelling at my dad and got more and more upset. Finally, she tried to jump out of the car when it was going down the highway. My dad pulled over and she jumped out and ran to a lake and jumped in. My dad went in after her and carried her back to the car. After that, my brother and I had to hold her car door lock down, so that she wouldn't try to jump out while the car was moving. The next town we got to, she demanded to get out and ride the bus home.

We drove around until we found a bus stop, but it was Sunday and the busses weren't running. We couldn't find a bus schedule, so we sat in the heat and just waited for hours for a bus to come. Several times, my mom got out of the car and took off and my dad chased her in and out of stores and businesses. Finally, late in the afternoon, my mom realized that no bus was coming. She calmed down and we drove home in complete silence. We never had anything to eat for the entire day. Once we had returned home, late that night, she demanded that my dad take her to find a motel. They came back together and for the next two weeks, she stayed in her bedroom.

That is the most extreme example of my mother's irrational rage, but she often locked herself in the bathroom and threatened to commit suicide after an argument with my dad. She would shake the razor blades or the aspirin bottle. Many times, on family outings to get ice cream or go to the movies, she would get mad at something and jump out of the car and my dad would drive along beside her and repeat over and over again, "Get in the car," Until she finally got back in.

When I was 11 years old, I called Fort Logan Mental Hospital and asked them what I needed to do to get my mother committed to the hospital. I told them she was threatening to commit suicide. They told me that she had to actually do something to hurt herself or someone else before they could take her involuntarily.

By the time I was a teenager, my father had a master's degree and was a high school teacher, coach, and referee. He worked as a mailman for Sears on Saturdays. I began imitating my father's work ethic at age 14. In school, I volunteered in the special education classrooms, kept stats for the athletic teams, joined several school clubs, and was very active.

At the age of 15, I ran away from home for about three months. I stayed at the home of one of my school friends whose parents were both teachers. I couldn't believe how nice they treated each other and how much love and affection they showed for their kids. It was another awakening about how other families show each other they care.

In college, I earned a Bachelor's Degree with a double major in three years while working full-time and holding down 3 jobs in the summers. My workaholism was in full swing. I was running from reality. One time, I remember I was going through some tough times at school and feeling particularly lonely. I hadn't called my parents for several weeks and decided to wait and see how long it would take for them to contact me. After waiting 3 months, I called my mother. She told me that she and my dad had separated and were divorcing, she had just had a complete hysterectomy, and she was selling our family home. She had thrown away all of my belongings and keepsakes.

That was a huge awakening for me that my parents didn't have any feeling of connectedness to me. They had consciously kept me out of three major life events. My dad told me that he had been staying in the marriage for years because of my brother and I. My brother had moved out recently at the age of 16, so my dad felt he could finally leave. This was only the beginning of many long lapses of contact I would have with my mother.

Right after college graduation, I married a man much like my mother. He was angry, critical, controlling, and never quite satisfied with much of anything I did. He was also a mean and abusive alcoholic. I was comfortable with this, because I had grown up with similar treatment, so I decided that I would rise to the challenge.

He wanted to be a lawyer and I thought this would be a perfect job for me. I could help him to reach his dreams and do something worthwhile. I helped him with his research, critiqued his class presentations, edited his papers, helped him prepare for tests, and earned my Master's Degree at the same time. All the while, I taught school full-time.

We both graduated in three years and returned to his small hometown to begin our family. He believed that we should both contribute equally to the family income, so I taught school while we added three children to our family. The last three years of our marriage, I quit teaching to help him part-time in his law office. During that time, I started a consignment store, an economic development corporation, and held down a part-time job as a diversion counselor for youth offenders. Luckily, there were many wonderful surrogate mothers who came forward to help me to raise my children. This was only through God's grace.

At one point, I took my children and went to a

safe house for battered women. I went back home after two weeks, but this was the beginning of the end of our marriage. My husband's drinking was getting worse and I was feeling more afraid and out of control in my life. I was working about 90 hours a week and I was really unhappy. I started going for counseling and reading self-help books. The counselor suggested that I go for a 2-week in-patient treatment for co-dependency. I started reading about co-dependency and took a couple of weekend long courses.

At the end of the courses, the counselors also recommended that I do a residential 2-week program for co-dependency. This 2-week program would turn into a 9-month treatment program for an eating disorder in Illinois and far away from my family. The residential treatment program really changed my life. I learned how to love and parent myself, how to trust God, how to talk to God, and most importantly how let go and listen to God. I am so grateful for the time and opportunity that I had to heal and process my past hurts and my faulty thinking.

At the end of the treatment, the treatment center said they had misdiagnosed my case and that I did not have an eating disorder and they did not charge me anything. I continued with regular counseling and 12 step groups for another 15 years and focused on my work addiction and my chronic depression.

By the time I had completed 5 months of treatment and 4 months in a women's halfway house, I was sure that I could not return to my marriage. I hired an attorney and filed for divorce. Even though (prior to my treatment) my husband had spent very little time parenting the children, he fought for sole custody.

He teamed up with a corrupt divorce attorney, who eventually was disbarred, who did everything imaginable to intimidate me; from stealing my checks and declaring I was violating a court order to dragging the court battle out for years.

They had all of our property devalued and reported it was all worthless, so I walked away from my home of 17 years with literally nothing. With me out of the picture, my husband turned to his children as his victims. He was abusing and severely neglecting them, so I turned him in to social services over 25 times. Besides having to take a parenting class and do some counseling, there were no consequences for his actions.

Confident that there would be no way that I would

lose a custody battle, I went through two custody evaluations, with an agency I would learn later was associated with my husband. Needless to say, after three years of legal battles and $20,000 in fees, I lost the custody of my children. I was devastated and went into a deep depression. I wasn't suicidal, but I had lost the will to live.

By Rumi

God turns you from one feeling to another and teaches by means of opposites, so that you will have two wings to fly, not one.
This discipline and rough treatment are a furnace to extract the silver from the dross.
This testing purifies the gold by boiling the scum away.

My children were my whole life and they were the only reason that I was trying to heal. I could not imagine this scenario. I could not figure out what God wanted me to do. I stayed in counseling and gradually began to feel better, but it was a long and painful road to recovery. Being there for my kids was the only reason I existed at this point. God was good to my kids, in the bigger picture. He found a very special woman to help raise my children. Together, we did the best we could to give them the love they deserved, while their father spent most of his time at work or at the local tavern. He continued to abuse them, both physically and emotionally, and I often felt helpless to do anything about it.

The entire ordeal was extremely hard on them and I am sure it affected each of them deeply. I did what I could to nurture them on the weekends, summers, and holidays, but I will always regret that they had to endure so much suffering.

About three years later, I began a doctoral program in education and graduated 10 years later. During this time, I started writing grants and was awarded a large three-year grant to serve high-risk high school students and potential dropouts: it was called The Poudre Transition Center and is still in operation in Fort Collins.

A year later and with some financial help from a former boss, two partners and I started an alternative high school for youth on probation. We called it Choices. It operated for two years until the local probation department started their own program based upon our model. Next, I wrote a proposal to the

State of Colorado to operate a day-treatment center for youth offenders called Beaucaire Youth Services. Beaucaire was in operation for 13 years and served about 300 youth.

My childhood experiences helped me to understand and work with these youth offenders. Many of them had traumatic childhoods, parents who were absent or not able to parent, and many of the youth struggled with their own mental illnesses.

Most of them suffered much more than I ever did. My struggles seemed mild in comparison. I am grateful to have been able to see their desire to grow and transform their lives. They were so strong, their recoveries were truly amazing miracles. The relationships I had with these youth were powerful experiences in faith.

I am so grateful that God opened my eyes and pulled me to Him. I don't know if I would have realized the need for God in my life, if I hadn't suffered as much as I did. I had my priorities and beliefs all upside down. My sorrows created a deeper, more sincere yearning for love that I equated to a yearning for God's love. The abuse and loss of control I experienced in my childhood and in my marriage taught me the submission and detachment that I would understand as an adult and would use to focus on loving God and detaching from worldly distractions. My pain taught me to have compassion for others who were struggling.

My life experiences have made me feel like I have lived several lifetimes wrapped up in one. I had so many lessons to learn that I had many scenarios in which to learn them. I had many teachers; the two biggest ones were my mother and my husband. They were a mirror for the person I was becoming. I am really grateful for their tough lessons.

The Guest House
By Rumi

This being human is a guest house.
Every morning a new arrival.
A joy, a depression, a meanness.
Some momentary awareness comes
As an unexpected visitor.
Welcome and entertain them all!
Even if they're a crowd of sorrows,
Who violently sweep your house
Empty of its furniture,
Still, treat each guest honorably.
He may be cleaning you out

For some new delight.
The dark thought, the shame, the malice,
Meet them at the door laughing,
And invite them in.
Be grateful for whoever comes,
Because each has been sent
As a guide from beyond.

Author Bio

Lynette is currently on the faculty at Front Range Community College and at the Community College of Denver. She also operates a publishing company, McClain Productions, which offers publishing, editing, ghost writing, formatting and designing of books and book covers.

She has a PhD in Education from Colorado State University, a Masters Degree in Educational Psychology from the University of Nebraska and a Bachelors Degree in Elementary Education and Special Education from the University of Northern Colorado.

Lynette taught English, reading and math in the public schools in Colorado and Nebraska for over 20 years. In 1992, she started Directions Unlimited: Youth Vocational Center, a non-profit school and treatment center for high-risk youth which operated under the name of Beaucaire Youth Services. Beaucaire provided mentoring, counseling and therapy, monitoring, housing, and schooling to paroling and high-risk youth.

The center focused on sex offenders in the later years. She also formed the Sedgwick County Christmas Store, a consignment store for local craftsman and artisans which is still in operation; Sedgwick County Cottage Industry, which was operated by senior citizens; and the SCORE: Sedgwick County Organization to Revitalize the Economy, which was a community organization promoting economic development.

She was voted Woman of the Year in 1985 by the Julesburg Chapter of Business and Professional Women. She lives in Longmont where she is writing several books.

"My passion is helping others to see the good that is around them. I do this by connecting people via events, and recently via digital technology. When I keep my heart open, I can see people in need. My talents are being able to see solutions, responding to the need and solving parts of the problem. I am a connector, a conduit for good."
   — Gael Sylvia Pullen

Gael Sylvia Pullen

⮞ 6 ⮜

"Able to See Solutions"

By Gael Sylvia Pullen

To this day, I still hear the voices of my father, here on earth and in heaven. Few childhood memories are as profound as the routine of our nightly bedtime prayers, hearing the voices of our parents as they kneeled at our bedside. In a rank and file order of my eldest brother, then me, and then three younger siblings, we closed our eyes and spoke to a very real spiritual Father. As simply as "Now I lay me, down to sleep, I pray the Lord my soul to keep," the power of prayer was planted in my heart along with a deep awareness of a power source that is real.

As the eldest daughter, I was often introduced as the timid one. I was a shy, observant girl with a spirit of curiosity, and those gifts have been the basis for understanding a loving Father. He receives us as we are. I only need to quiet myself, be still and I can hear. I can hear His guidance for the daily routine activities of being a wife, mother, business owner and creator.

The advantage of being both shy and observant is that I have learned to be patient with others. I can patiently hear what may not be spoken out loud. I can observe eye movement, body language and the tears pooling in the wells of someone's eyes, even though they may be pretending that all is well in their world. These are honored gifts that allow me an opportunity to love.

How did I learn to be observant? As only a grandparent can teach it, I learned it from my grandmother. Sitting at her side listening to her tell stories of generations gone by, or folding laundry, peeling apples, driving to church, I heard with fascination every detailed description she shared. She gave us the gift of her stories.

She was my paternal grandmother, and another gift she gave us was learning to create our own happy memories. She would entertain five grandchildren by preparing southern fried chicken, gravy, rice, salad, peach cobbler and homemade lemonade, piling all of us into her car with picnic blankets, and taking us all to the local train station where we would observe passengers coming and going.

She crafted tales about each unsuspecting character in the equivalent of a 1970's reality T.V. show. She would draw our hearts' attention to facial expressions: the tight lips of a middle-aged woman, the flushed face of a man seeing a woman, the stride or bounce in a walk, the lack of acknowledgement or the length of a warm embrace.

Within each of these moments from the lives of others and the generations that shaped each of them, I learned to see God within us all. I also learned to notice His absence. On a daily basis, I have role models: the people who enter my life for a moment or longer and model a quality that reflects God, these are my role models.

To church-going Christians this may sound like a cliché, but I do find myself emulating the role models of the Bible. I can't think of better examples of life lessons. As I read and re-read passages in the Bible, details seem to jump off the page into the quiet, sacred spaces of my heart, only to resurface later as reminders of God's presence.

I have had the wonderful experience of living abroad. I encourage everyone to consider leaving the comfort zone of the familiar and to experience first hand the greatness of our God in this vast world. Memories of my Japanese mother are side-by-side with memories of my birth mother, Swiss mom and many others who have nurtured my soul. Each had a role in my life and characteristics worthy of copying: love, patience and creativity.

Their love of ministry as a wife, mother and friend required much patience. Each had a unique ability to create beauty from the simple moments of preparing a lunch or a family dinner. This same loving patience was evident in their community-building work. Their involvement became my involvement.

Having mothers' love from around the world created within me a sense of global community, a feeling of belonging and ability to contribute no matter where I am. Simple activities, such as hosting a neighborhood Fourth of July apple bobbing contest in the suburbs of Tokyo, have led to hosting 5,000 girls in our program called Girls Fly! I seize every opportunity to express my gratitude for life through an expression of service to someone, no matter what or where their lives may have taken them. When people ask me, "How did you meet First Ladies of nations?" I can honestly respond by saying, "I loved the people in their countries first."

My husband and I formed our first non-profit in 1982 called "Better Communications, Inc." The mission was to increase the number of minority and low-income students participating in international exchange programs in association with science and technology.

A dreadful experience asking a corporate development officer at Union Oil for funding drove a stake through my soul. We vowed to never ever be on the "begging" end of the philanthropic spoon, but to learn all that we could to always be on the "giving" end of that spoon. Because he was an African-American man, I had assumed that he would immediately understand and support our effort. Much to my surprise, he placed his feet on his desk, soles of his shoes in my face, leaned back in his chair and proceeded to tell me of the many proud international experiences his two sons had been given. He also informed me, "That the best thing you can do for those people is help them finish high school without getting pregnant and going to jail."

A lesson my mother always taught us is, "Never assume anything about anyone." Within a matter of seconds, a defining moment in my life would take place: I had to decide if I would stay and try to persuade him to write us a check, being further humiliated, or seize hold of the dignity and strength associated with the legacy of generations before me.

I rose from the chair, gathered my presentation and purse, and the shy, observant little girl became a valiant warrior of faith, slaying the spirit of fear by saying, "I am pleased for your sons, but shame on you to think others are of lesser value." I walked out. Holding the invisible hand of God as I dropped twenty -three stories in the elevator, I drove to my husband's job and cried.

My life, my faith, and my work have remained consistent through the years: our God is an ever present help, and because He is greater and I am a vessel of His plan, rest assured He will do His good work through me whether I am up or down.

My passion is helping others to see the good that is around them. I do this by connecting people via events, and recently via digital technology. When

I keep my heart open, I can see people in need. My talents are being able to see solutions, responding to the need and solving parts of the problem.

I am a connector, a conduit for good. Through the years this has shaped how I lead in business and in opportunities to influence policies at the U.S.-Mexico border, I once spent ten months researching the methods of making large philanthropic commitments. I attended multiple meetings with attorneys, donors, and institutions. You name it; I read it and met with them. I executed contracts completely at peace with the decisions prayerfully made.

At one point, I signed a small Memorandum of Understanding, only to have the party threaten to sue me for not meeting a gift deadline, which they had agreed might be a tight deadline! I was stunned! To this day, I remain puzzled and ponder the question, "What did I miss, Lord?"

The same answer keeps resurfacing, "Nothing. Sometimes you just can't see the heart and motives of people." In these moments, it can be hard to trust again: Hard to trust my decision-making processes, my advisors, my faith, and my instincts. However, I always choose to look for the good and to keep taking all things to the Knower of All Hearts.

In the quiet of the early morning, I am often awakened by a heavenly spirit's whisper. I am learning to listen to that still, small voice preparing me for the work ahead. Sometimes, I long to see more Christians own their strength in God and step forward as Benaiah did. I long for more leaders to pray BIG, BOLD prayers of faith, as Jabez did. Sometimes, I long to see Christians close their mouths and open their hearts, demonstrating the power of a personal experience of faith.

Press Bio

Global technology spokesperson for women and girls, Gael Sylvia is the founder of Girls Fly! and Sylvia Global Media Network (SGMN). With the First Lady of Belize, she is the co-sponsor of the upcoming *"First Ladies of Nations Financial Summit."* Channeling quality, trustworthy content, she uses her global broadcasting digital network to serve as a sphere of influence for women and girls around the world.

Author Bio

Gael Sylvia is a pioneering businesswoman, a prolific speaker, and an ardent philanthropist, resulting in her membership in Women Moving Millions. Her life's goal is to empower and inspire all to see the good that is around us. Acting out of her core values, she is the founder of Sylvia Global Media Network, a global broadcasting digital platform that serves as a sphere of influence for women and girls around the world. Channeling quality, trustworthy content, Sylvia Global Media Network is a referral source of amazing women and enlightened men.

Founder of Girls Fly!, she hosted 5,000 girls in Belize in June, 2013, to an experience associated with their dreams. She is the former owner of Ghail Media

Group – the largest brokered Spanish-radio broadcast in northeastern Ohio, and Charis Real Estate – the largest minority-owned (revenue generated) commercial real estate brokerage firm in southern California during the mid-80s. She is a recently retired, award-winning McDonald's franchisee.
"I have always wanted to create a place of influence that would amplify the diverse voices of women and girls and the incredible work being done by image activists globally and by women's funding networks from donors to grantees.

Gael Sylvia Pullen is a Co-Sponsor of the First Ladies Financial Summit working in collaboration with Mrs. Barrow, First Lady of Belize, as an advocate for women and girls advancing Mrs. Barrow's specific goals. Guided by Mrs. Barrow's vision as a First Lady, they work on behalf of women via Mrs. Barrow's Office of the Special Envoy for Women & Children, Ministry of Human Development (Belize), the government of Belize and partner affiliates.

At a 2010 meeting she convened with the former U.S. Surgeon General at Canyon Ranch in Tucson, Arizona, with philanthropic and global corporate leaders, Gael Sylvia's passion met purpose as she became the leading proponent of a "Global Call To Action for Women and Girls' Health – The First Ladies of Influence Campaign." Lending support to global influencers at all levels of society is a significant part of her philanthropic model, sharing a lifetime of experiences, resources and relationships to unite and support one another. Her soul desires to elevate the influence of underrepresented women and girls and to unite them for the common good.

"Re-imaging what is commonly associated with wealth, the word philanthropist, and revealing alternative models of what success truly is, Sylvia Global is the connective tissue for all the good perpetuated in our lives at every level. From the least expected places to a refreshing perspective from the most familiar, here is an opportunity to hear and see added dimension to what women's work truly is."

"I see women and girls' financial health and philanthropy as inexorably linked. To create healthy women and girls, we need to re-imagine the word philanthropy and our place in the charity equation. It is often assumed that the recipient of philanthropy is only capable of being on the receiving end. But there's this other side to women and girls – the Women Moving Millions side. We are capable of being incredible change agents."
– Inland Valley Newspaper
January 6. 2012

"WHOEVER LOVES HIS BROTHER LIVES IN THE LIGHT." (1John 2:10A)

"I lead others by offering them opportunities to grow with me. I am a practical theologian, so I believe wholeheartedly in going where people are to do ministry. I believe in telling the whole truth of the gospel of Jesus Christ and not watering it down."

– Reverend Edna Morgan

Reverend Edna Morgan

~ 7 ~

"Privilege and Honor to Lead"

By Reverend Edna Morgan

My parents were from poor families. My Mom taught us the Lord's Prayer and the 23rd Psalm, when we were very young. We always attended Sunday school and Methodist summer camp at Aldersgate. She said our prayers with us before we went to bed and we said verses before meals. We enjoyed Vacation Bible School every summer.

I had a lovely childhood with lots of outdoor play, lots of reading in the home, and lots of love. Dad loved picnics, so we had a lot of neighborhood picnics where my dad would cook and all of my friends would come to my house for fellowship and a great meal.

My dad loved his family and his community. As a child, I remember my Dad lifting my friends, my sister, and me in the air every evening when he arrived home from work. He taught my sister and me how to swim, ride our bikes, and fish. My mom thought he treated us too much like boys and she wanted us to be more ladylike.

My dad wanted us to enjoy our childhood and he was not as interested in getting us to do our chores as my mom was. Both of my parents were fun to be around. I learned what unconditional love meant from my parents and the close-knit community of my formative years.

I also learned how to share, care for others, have fun, work hard, live in harmony with others, and follow Christian principles. Our loving community was within and around Watson Boulevard. Every adult served like surrogate moms and dads and every child was like a brother or sister. We celebrated every holiday and enjoyed nature. My family, church and community helped give me a good Christian foundation for healthy living and community life.

In high school, my favorite teacher was my piano and math teacher, Mrs. Marjorie Kirby. She was very strict; however, she treated everybody the same. My love for playing piano was nurtured by her. She taught me how to play hymns and classical music. She also took me to musicals in Little Rock. This joy for music is still with me today and I have been playing piano for worship services since I was twelve years old. I also learned to play the flute and organ.

My godparents, Mr. and Mrs. Fulton Walker, were very instrumental in my life. In fact, my godfather is still very significant in my life. He has always been there for me. I can call on him at any time for assistance, for advice, and just for a casual, fun conversation. He is like a spiritual adviser to me. Quite significant is the fact that my godfather gave me away when I married my high school sweetheart, David Morgan, in 1972.

My godmother awakened my passion for learning, particularly reading, and she always remembered special occasions. Mr. Walker's daughter and son-in-law, Wanda and Robert Truesdale, are like sister and brother to me. They are also wonderfully consistent contributors to our non-profit programs, along with my best friend, Georgette Wiley.

My dad died when I was twelve years old and in sixth grade. My sister and I were awakened from sleep by our mom during the night, who told us that our dad had been in a car accident. We prayed and stayed together awaiting news about how my dad was. Later that morning, my mom got a call that my dad had died instantly. All of the people in both cars had died.

I was very sad. I remember my sister, my mom, and I hugging each other and crying. I remember our wonderful neighbors, including the Caines, Trammells, Johnsons, Clemmons and others bringing over lots of food and staying in contact with us for what seemed like weeks after the accident.

I was angry with God for letting my dad die. In time, God healed my pain, and I learned to take joy in the wonderful times that I had spent with my dad. My mom died during my first year of college. Mrs. Trammell called to tell me. I told her she could not be telling the truth because my mom was not sick. She explained to me that I needed to come home right away. I asked her how my mom had died. She explained that my mom had been shot.

Later, we were told that my mom's death was an accident. She was on her way home from a school conference in Little Rock. It was believed that she was the victim of a stray bullet from maybe a hunter's gun somewhere on the highway from Little Rock to Pine Bluff. We later discovered that her second husband, a marriage she had had annulled, transported her in his car to our local hospital. Many believe he shot my mom. Ironically, over 40 years later, my husband and I started our city's Parents of Murdered Children support group.

Her death was such a shock for us. We were numb for quite some time. We managed to get through the funeral; however, I do not think we really began to grieve until we spent the first Thanksgiving and Christmas without our mom. Again our community and family, my Maternal Grandmother Roxie, Aunt Ernestine and Uncle Payton were wonderful walking with us through this trauma. After some time, our faithful God healed us and we remember our mom with fondness.

In the absence of my biological parents, God gave me two additional parents, my mom's sister and her husband, Mr. and Mrs. Elbert Payton. They played very significant roles in my life and the lives of my family from 1970 onward. They were marvelous Christian parents to my husband and me and grandparents to our children.

I married my high school sweetheart, Reverend David Morgan, in 1972. I love David for his kindness and compassion. He grew up in a Christian family, as well. He is a wonderful soul mate and a great friend, father and grandfather. When we make major decisions, we discuss how each of us feels and we pray. I am blessed to have him in my life.

Some of my educational accomplishments include graduating from Merrill High School, Pine Bluff, as valedictorian. I received a bachelor's degree in Music Education from Hendrix College, Conway, AR, in 1974, with honors; a master's degree in Educational Supervision and Administration from Roosevelt University, Chicago, IL, in 1982 with honors; and my master of divinity with honors in May of 2005.

My love for learning came from my parents and I believe one never gets too old to learn. God keeps giving me new insights through God's Word and through the wisdom from other believers, from family, and from friends. I will always be open to grow in the knowledge and grace of our Lord and Savior Jesus Christ. I have a passion for the study of the Bible and growing in general and imparting to others what I have learned.

As a leader, I serve as a crime victims' chaplain where I co-chair the ministries of Healing Place, our non-profit, 501c3. We work with several volunteers and agencies' employees within Jefferson and Pulaski Counties. We care for victims of crime, providing advocacy support, crises pastoral counseling, support group meetings, training, information dissemination, and referral and reparation services. We also provide life skills training for families at our church and at a local housing authority community center. We operate a summer youth camp, too. In addition, we provide fellowship game nights for seniors at two assisted living facilities. Our plates are full and we love what we do. When God calls you, God equips you.

I lead others by offering them opportunities to grow with me. I am a practical theologian, so I believe wholeheartedly in going where people are to do ministry. I believe in telling the whole truth of the gospel of Jesus Christ and not watering it down.

The Great Commission says, "Go ye therefore," so we have to go where the people are to share with them the love of Jesus. If we do not go where they are, how can we get close enough to them to build relationships so that they can become a part of God's dynamic plan

for humanity? When we lift up our Savior, our Savior will do the drawing. Our job is to be ready to share our gifts, our financial resources, our churches, our homes, and all other resources which God has loaned us but for a moment until we reach our heavenly home.
My husband and I dreamed of returning home and giving back to the community where we had been blessed as children. God fulfilled our dream.

We worked on each detail of our dream until the day our first summer camp drew near. We prepared our non-profit documentation with the help of our local university staff. We got our 501c3 status and started networking within our city to find partners to help with resources.

We put summer camp dates on our calendar, got staff from other agencies to help us, and facilitated our first camp for at-risk and disadvantaged children in 2005. We started with 20 children and here we are eight years later having served over 1500 children in Pine Bluff, Arkansas, and surrounding areas.
My District Superintendent, C. E. McAdoo at that time, noticed a letter in his e-mail looking for crime victim chaplains, so he shared the letter with me.
I applied for the position and became the first crime victims' chaplain in Arkansas. My husband joined me

later in that ministry. We have been serving victim survivors since 2005. It was another one of God's gifts, crime victim chaplaincy, that is. I applied for a federal grant, one of one hundred twenty six applicants, and got one of 26 grants awarded. We have had that federal grant, Victims of Crime Act, since 2005 – another one of God's incredible gifts.

God birthed our Parents of Murdered Children (POMC) support group three years ago, our life skills training five years ago, and our assisted living ministry four years ago. Our God is an incredibly creative God, who is willing to lead us as long as we're willing to follow.

All ministries have been incredibly wonderful. I believe we receive more than we give. If you are interested in replicating any of our ministries, please give me a call. I'm willing to share our story with all who are interested in hard yet incredibly rewarding work.

I would not do anything differently. I believe all that we have gone through has been for a reason, for our learning. I do not think of hurdles as mistakes. Hurdles are simply life. The life of a Christian is challenging. It has its peaks and valleys. There is no way of getting around that truth; yet, "every valley shall be raised up, every mountain and hill made low; the rough ground shall become level, the rugged places a plain (Isaiah 40:4)." You just have to learn to "wait for the Lord; be strong and take heart and wait for the Lord (Psalm 27:14)."

You just have to have faith. I cannot say that my contribution alone has impacted others. My agency, my donors, my volunteers, and my staff have impacted others with me. I cannot take credit for the work of a community of believers whom I cannot even number. Examples are the many victim survivors who have come through our agency for help and have found a new normal, a way to continue their life with healing and hope. Many become our volunteers and find strength to "pass it on."

I cannot number the children who have gone to our summer camp, who would not have an opportunity to receive loving care at a camp where they did not realize that they were learning coping skills such as how to be resilient and self-confident along with team building skills. I cannot number the families who have learned from us and we learned from them about how to live resiliently and how to raise productive and caring children during this new millennium era in which we live and move and have our being. I cannot tell you the number of victim survivors and citizens of our community who have been comforted by our annual memorial services, where memorial walls of our homicide losses are exhibited; care, compassion and fellowship are flowing; and, prayers shawls made by Arkansas United Methodist Women are given to each homicide survivor family. I can say that it is a privilege and honor to lead in these ministries. Each day is an adventure and each day God is with us leading and directing us as we practice Christian living.

My involvement in these ministries has made me more compassionate. My involvement in these ministries has kept me in my prayer closet daily interceding for others. My involvement in these ministries has kept me humble and has kept me learning and open to new ways of doing ministry. My involvement in these ministries is still stretching me and calling me to learn more about Jesus and to implement what I learn for the benefit of others and my own spiritual growth.

My vision is to continue to hear God's direction for my life so that I can work in the vineyard on my God-given assignment until He calls me home to live in the heavens forever. I believe the ministries that

God has and will give my husband, our volunteers, and me are yet being created in the atmosphere and when God knows we are ready for the next step in this journey of faith God will reveal to us what God wants us to do and we'll walk through another door into service wherever and with whomever God calls us to reach.

The source of our vision is God, our Lord and Savior Jesus Christ, the Comforting Holy Spirit alive and moving everyday in our lives. Thank you, Lord God, for the body of Christ and for your precious revelations within our small part of your huge, loving plan for humanity.

Author Bio

Reverend Morgan accepted Christ as her personal savior at age 12 at St. James United Methodist Church in Pine Bluff and returned home in 1999 to continue a legacy of giving to her community that she learned there as a child. She graduated valedictorian from Merrill High School, Pine Bluff, Arkansas, in May 1970. She received her Bachelor's degree in Music Education from Hendrix College, Conway, AR, in 1974 and her Master's degree in Educational Supervision and Administration from Roosevelt University, Chicago, IL in 1982.

She received her Master of Divinity degree in 2004 from Memphis Theological Seminary and completed Clinical Pastoral Education as a chaplain at JRMC in May of 2005. She became an Ordained Elder, AR UMC in 2007, certified AR preventionist in 2009, and nationally certified chaplain in February of 2008. She is working on a master's in counseling at the University of Arkansas, Little Rock.

She retired from the federal government after 26 years of service both across the US and overseas. In 2005, God opened doors for Reverend Edna to work as Crime Victims' Chaplain of the Arkansas Conference of the United Methodist Church, along with her husband, Reverend David Morgan, under their non-profit, Christian Retreat Center, the Healing Place Ministries. This ministry is located at First United Methodist Church (FUMC) in Pine Bluff. The retreat center at 8309 Old Warren Road is used for Summer Camp, family reunions, institutional and organizational retreats, weddings, and receptions.

Rev. Edna served as Associate Pastor of FUMC, Pine Bluff, for three years from 2009-2012. Her organizational affiliations and volunteerism include: Order of Elders of the UMC, Association of Professional Chaplains, former appointed member of the Governor's Alcohol and Drug Abuse Coordinating Council, Federally Employed Women, Kiwanis, Pine Bluff Prayer Community, Adult/Older Adult Task Force, Volunteer Chaplain (Pine Bluff Arsenal), UMW, RSVP and AARP.

Her hobbies include cooking, crocheting, running, biking, swimming, reading, playing the piano, singing, and traveling. She has a passion for the study of the Bible, learning and growing in general, and imparting to others what she has learned.

Some of her fondest memories are of living in Los Alamitos, CA, Beltsville, MD, and Okinawa, Japan, while accompanying her husband during his 22 years in the U. S. Navy. She has also completed two Marine Corps Marathons, 26.2 miles of running non-stop.

Her current goals are to complete the 501c3 non-profit retreat center, the Healing Place Ministries, a dream, which God gave to Revs. David and Edna before they moved back home to Pine Bluff.

She believes God has given each of us assignments here on earth which will bless others in mighty ways, because we are here to spread love, joy, peace, and harmony. One of her favorite verses is "Do not merely listen to the word, and so deceive yourselves. Do what it says." (James 1:22). She believes we can make our communities cohesive and effective for abundant 21st century living if we intentionally and consistently reach out and touch the hands of those who are in need. Reverend Morgan is committed to "To act justly and to love mercy and to walk humbly with your God." (Micah 6:8).

Her organization's name is: The Healing Place Ministries, Inc. There are two sites: 1) 8309 Old Warren Rd, Pine Bluff, AR 71603, and 2) 200 West Sixth, Pine Bluff, AR 71601. The latter is at First United Methodist Church, which has provided in-kind space to house the victim advocacy ministries. The office contact number is 870-535-0101 and the fax number is 870-535-0103. The website is healingplaceministries.com.

"LET THE LIGHT OF YOUR FACE SHINE UPON US, O LORD." (Psalm 4:6)

"When God gives me a new vision or project, I cannot complete it alone...I see the TPPM ministry as a big truck moving big loads. Many big wheels are needed to move this truck and the Lord is faithfully sending people to be those turning wheels."

— Yong Hui V. McDonald

Yong Hui *V.* McDonald

❧ 8 ❧

"Giver of the Vision"
By Yong Hui V. McDonald

Did I ever have a vision of becoming a minister or a spiritual leader as I was growing up? No. I did not have a clue what I would become, as I had neither goals in life nor a vision of helping others. I grew up in a family where survival was everyday life, not just materially, but emotionally and mentally as well. Then the Lord changed my life. He gave me visions and blessed me beyond my wildest imagination.

I was born in South Korea, raised in a family with a father who was not a Christian. He persecuted my mother because of her Christian faith. In spite of the persecution, my mother kept her faith and sent all of her children to church. I am forever grateful to my mother for planting the seed of faith in me. I was the second of five children. I had two brothers and two sisters. One younger sister was lost in a car accident. I had many struggles at home because of my father's alcoholism. His violent temper affected the whole family. I had to learn how to forgive my father, which I found possible only after his death. My father was definitely not a good role model. He was selfish and violent, which caused a lot of pain in the family.

Who were the mentors for my spiritual journey? My kind, loving, and gentle mother was a wonderful mentor for me. In fact, I believe that all of the blessings I have received in my ministry are because of her prayers. I learned from my parents that great leadership does not depend on a person's gender, but on their faith, godly character, commitment, and obedience to the Lord. If my mother had received a theological education, she would have been a great pastor. Even with no education, she influenced me positively and gave me the courage to serve the Lord.

Another person who helped me on my faith journey was my husband Keith, who passed away in 2008 in a car accident. I married Keith, a member of the American Air Force, in Korea in 1978, and we moved to the United States in 1979. We both attended Multnomah Bible College, where he was a constant help with my studies. He helped me prepare for ministry more than anyone else. He provided a stable Christian environment where I could study and experience healing from my childhood traumas.

Keith served as a United Methodist pastor. After God called me to the ministry, I decided to become a United Methodist minister as well. The United Methodist Church has many opportunities for ethnic minorities, including scholarships. I received scholarships as well as support, which I continue to receive as an extension minister.

Surprisingly, my husband Keith did not support my decision to go into the ministry. He wanted my support in his ministry as a pastor's wife, but when the time came to make a decision, I followed God's call to full-time ministry. Every week for 3 years, I commuted 430 miles each way from Buffalo, Wyoming, to Denver, Colorado, to attend the Iliff School of Theology. After I graduated, I planned to minister in Colorado. Keith realized that he couldn't change my heart, so we moved to Colorado. Even though he was reluctant to help me initially, in later years, he was supportive of my ministry. I am very grateful for this.

I had never thought about becoming a prison chaplain, but the Lord called me to the prison ministry. My older brother ran away from home at the age of 13 when my father started beating my mother. He wandered the streets, became involved with gangs, and eventually ended up in prison.

I vividly remember the day I visited him in prison. I was filled with grief, because I realized that if he had had a loving family, he wouldn't have run away from home or ended up incarcerated. I was flooded with tears, and when I saw him I couldn't say a word. I never went back to visit him again. It was heartbreaking to see him there. While he was incarcerated, I hoped that someone would introduce him to Jesus so he could be saved, find direction in his life, and have hope. Unfortunately, this never happened.

When I asked the Lord what He wanted me to do, He reminded me of what I had wanted to see come out of my older brother's incarceration. He asked me to do what I had wanted others to do for my brother – introduce people to Jesus. None of the churches that I attended had a prison ministry. In fact, I had no clue that America, a land of opportunity, had the largest prison population in the world – 2.3 million. Truly, the opportunities to minister to prisoners and their families are endless in this country.

My book ministry started while I was attending the Iliff School of Theology. I wrote *Journey With Jesus* before I started school, and I published it as a student at Iliff. I also wrote another book while in school and started distributing my books to prisons and to homeless shelters free of charge.

In 2003, after I began ministering as a chaplain at Adams County Detention Facility (ACDF), I realized that there was always a shortage of Christian books for the inmates. I got together with some friends and talked about how we could solve this problem. We decided that one person could not do it alone, so we started Transformation Project Prison Ministry (TPPM), a non-profit organization. TPPM started producing books full of prisoners' transformation stories, designed to help other prisoners. My first plan focused on ACDF inmates only, and I was going to publish 1,500 books. Then the Lord said,

"Your vision is too small." He challenged me to help other facilities and homeless shelters as well, so I published 10,000 copies. As of 2013, TPPM has distributed over 170,000 books to prisons and homeless shelters.

I also founded Griefpathway Ventures in 2010 to produce books for spiritual growth and healing. In 2011, the Lord also led me to start Veterans Twofish Foundation, another non-profit, to publish and distribute free books to prisoners, homeless shelters, and veterans' organizations.

In 2012, the Lord challenged me by saying, "If you were to save only one prisoner, would you start TPPM in Korea?" In 2013, I asked Reverend Lee Born in Korea to serve as the director of TPPM. TPPM has published 4,000 books in Korea to distribute in prisons. In January of 2014, TPPM was able to publish an additional 2,000 more books there. This has all been by God's grace. There are many who help with this project by volunteering to translate, illustrate, edit, fundraise, donate, and ship books. God is sending people to help with all of these book projects. Praise God!

What is my perspective on leadership? What inspires me these days? I have two inspiring pictures on the wall where I study. I have a picture of a beautiful sanctuary on the wall above my desk. It shows many beautiful wooden beams holding up the roof. This reminds me that I am only one of many beams and that many others are holding the roof together alongside me.

The other one is a picture of Jesus carrying a heavy cross, leaning on the ground from the heavy weight. An angel is trying to help Him to carry the cross. There are times when we cannot carry our cross by ourselves and we have to rely on each other. If we help carry each other's burdens, the weight of our own cross will be lighter.

Whenever God gives me a new vision or project to work on, I cannot even begin to complete it alone. Many people help me carry the cross of my ministry. One example of this is how TPPM was able to send one pallet (about 4,000 books) to the Twin Towers Correctional Facility in Los Angeles, California. The books include English, Spanish, and Korean versions. When the time came to send the pallet, I had many book projects underway and I didn't have the time or energy to do it. Amazingly, a wonderful volunteer named Phil took on the job of shipping. He did everything. Other volunteers continuously help me edit English and Korean books. Because of this, the ministry is growing. I praise God for all the leaders who work shoulder-to-shoulder with me and encourage each other.

Another example of how others help carry my burdens comes from January of 2014. TPPM printed 2,000 books in Korean for prisoners in South Korea. TPPM had to raise $5,000 to do this. I sent out an email sharing this project, to which the Chicago TPPM regional director responded. They raised all the funds! This is God's doing, so that I have the time to pray and work on the book projects the Lord has given me. I see the TPPM ministry as a big truck moving big loads. Many big wheels are needed to move this truck and the Lord is faithfully sending people to be those turning wheels.

The Lord is enlarging my vision. He asked me to reach out to leaders outside of prison, as well as to visit 500 churches to talk about prison revival. This gave me a new direction. I was already working with the American media, but the Korean book project gave me a reason to reach out to the Korean media and community as well. The Lord started opening doors to enable me to lead leadership training workshops and retreats.

I am working with the media to let others know about the prison ministry and how God is blessing prisoners through the book projects. I am amazed by the response of both Koreans and Americans to the media coverage of prison ministry. I have participated in many radio interviews, both in English and Korean. Korean Newspapers are also publishing my books. If God hadn't asked me to visit 500 churches, I wouldn't have thought about expanding my ministry through media coverage.

In 2012, God made it possible for me to go back to school to work towards a Doctor of Ministry at Asbury Theological Seminary. I am in the process of doing that with a full scholarship. The Lord is continuously encouraging me to envision ways to work with leaders in other countries, and now I am working with Asbury Seminary foreign students who want to be involved with TPPM.

God also changed the direction of my prayer life as well, so that He could share His heart and visions with me. The Lord called me to prayer many times, but on December 8, 2013, He called me to silent prayer. This became a refreshing time for me. The Lord asked me to spend less time with people and more time just listening to Him. He then began to give me a vision of the direction my ministry should take in the future. One of these visions led me to produce books to help poor children, whose parents cannot afford to buy books for them. This opened a new door for TPPM. Since they already reach out to homeless and incarcerated families, they can add the book project to help children without too much difficulty. A talented artist, Holly, volunteered to start this project. She is doing a great job. I am very encouraged.

Three weeks after I started silent prayer, the Lord also helped me to write a book, *Journey With Jesus Two,* which is an answer to my prayers. I had been asking the Lord if He would help me write a book as powerful as *Journey With Jesus* ever since I first made the decision to follow my calling to serve Jesus, which occurred after I wrote that book.

Journey With Jesus Two taught me how to recognize the importance of silent prayer and listening. When I listen, the Lord shares His heart. My future visions and dreams of ministry are all related to what He shares with me. I am learning about God's love and grace through this silent prayer. It has also helped me to develop a habit of prayer, which I needed badly.

What did I learn about God after I started my ministry? I learned more about His love and power. At the beginning of my ministry, when I asked the Lord, "What shall I preach?" He would answer, "Tell them I love them." This is the answer I still get today when I ask the Lord what I need to preach. God's love is what people need to hear. When I tell them God's message for them is that He loves them, some people break down and cry. Why? These people are in desperate need of someone to remind them that God loves them.

If we can learn more about God's love, we will become more loving as well as better equipped to handle difficult situations. I also preach that God not only loves them, but doesn't condemn them. This message is important for those wearing prisoner's clothes who know that society looks down on them. God's great love and power breaks that bondage of shame and guilt.

I lead about ten worship services every week at ACDF and, even though I have interns who help me from time to time, I have led about 5,000 worship services so far. I have gotten a glimpse of what God can do through worship services where the Holy Spirit touches people. I have seen people who have had no direction and were living a destructive lifestyle change to become people who are so filled with God's love that they reach out to other inmates. God has blessed me by leading me to see a spiritual revival in prisons. An extremely powerful manifestation of the Holy Spirit can be felt in these places. Many people wonder where God's power is. God's healing power can appear wherever people are hurting. I am thankful that the Lord has blessed me to see this where I minister.

Interestingly, God gave me unconditional love for prisoners. It doesn't matter who they are. If they are wearing prison clothes, my love for them is there. I know God planted love in my heart for prisoners because they are hurting people. I am willing to help them, and I don't even look at their charges because it only encourages a judgmental attitude. I am there to share God's love and forgiveness. That is my focus.

Responding to God's call to ministry was one of the best things that has happened in my life. I regret that I didn't go into the ministry sooner. I feel more fulfillment through the ministry than with any other job I have ever had. The Lord has filled me with so much joy because of it. Now, I don't want to miss out on any opportunity to serve God. In fact, if anyone is struggling to respond to the call to ministry, I would say to them, "Obey the Lord and you will see miracles." When I follow God's visions, I see many miracles. His grace is definitely sufficient for me.

Author Bio

Reverend Yong Hui V. McDonald, Founder and co-Executive Director of Transformation Project Prison Ministry (TPPM) and United Methodist minister, was born and grew up in South Korea. She married Keith McDonald and came to the United States in 1979. She graduated from Multnomah University with a Bachelors degree and attended Iliff School of Theology, graduating with Master's of Divinity degree.

She began her prison ministry in 1999 while attending Iliff, and in 2003, she started working as a Chaplain at Adams County Detention Facility (ACDF) in Brighton, Colorado.

She called her prison ministry "Transformation Project Prison Ministry" with the goal of addressing a shortage of inspirational books for inmates. She started publishing her own books under "Griefpathways Ventures LLC" and "Veterans Twofish Foundation," with all of the books distributed at no cost to help prisoners, the homeless, and veterans in need of the love of Christ and His healing power.

She currently is actively promoting prison ministry among Koreans especially Korean-American United Methodist Women. She has given presentations about prison ministry in many churches, lead grief workshops and retreats.

TPPM was featured at General Conference of the United Methodist Church in 2008. She was one of the speakers for a "Women Making Peace" leadership training with the Korean United Methodist Women in 2013.

She has written 24 English books, 10 of which have been translated into Korean; produced 2 DVDs' and has had two books translated into Spanish. She is currently working on her Doctor of Ministry from Asbury Theological Seminary.

Her most recent books include a collection of stories by prison ministry Chaplains and volunteers entitled *Lost but Not Forgotten: Life Behind Prison Walls*, and a book entitled *Loving God, 100 Daily Meditations and Prayers*.

"FOR GOD SO LOVED THE WORLD THAT HE GAVE HIS ONE AND ONLY SON, THAT WHOEVER BELIEVES IN HIM SHALL NOT PARISH BUT HAVE ETERNAL LIFE."

(John 3:16)

Appendices

An Invitation

Do you have an empty heart that doesn't seem to be filled by anyone or anything? God can fill your empty heart with His love and forgiveness. Do you feel your life has no meaning, no direction, no purpose, and you don't know where to turn to find the answers? It's time to turn to God. That's the only way you will understand the meaning and the purpose of your life. You will find direction that will lead you to fulfillment and joy. Is your heart broken and hurting, and you don't know how to experience healing?

Until we meet Christ in our hearts, we cannot find the peace and healing that God can provide. Jesus can help heal your broken heart. If you don't have a relationship with Christ, this is an opportunity for you to accept Jesus into your heart so you can be saved, and be able to find peace and healing from God. Here is a prayer if you are ready to accept Jesus:

"Dear Jesus, I surrender my life and everything to you. I give you all my pain, fear, regret, resentment, anger, worry, and concerns that overwhelm me. I am a sinner. I need your forgiveness. Please come into my heart and my life and forgive all my sins. I believe that you died for my sins and that you have plans for my life. Please heal my broken heart and bless me with your peace and joy. Help me to cleanse my life, so I can live a godly life. Help me to understand your plans for my life and help me to obey you. Fill me with the Holy Spirit, and guide me so I can follow your way. I pray this in Jesus' name. Amen."

Resources

Transformation Project Prison Ministry (TPPM)

The Transformation Project Prison Ministry, a 501(c) (3) non-profit organization, produces, publishes books and DVDs and distributes them to prisons, jails, and homeless shelters nationwide. TPPM produces *Maximum Saints* books and DVDs containing transformation stories of inmates at Adams County Detention Facility, in Brighton, Colorado. Your donation is 100% tax deductible. TPPM has distributed over 170,000 books and DVDs free of charge. If you would like to be a partner in this very important mission of reaching out to prisoners and homeless, or want to know more about this project, please visit them online at: www.maximumsaints.org. You can donate on line or you can write a check addressed to:

Transformation Project Prison Ministry
5209 Montview Boulevard
Denver, CO 80207

Facebook: http://tinyurl.com/yhhcp5g
Email: tppm.ministry@gmail.com

Transformation Project Prison Ministry was started in Korea. Contact: Rev. Lee Born, Director of TPPM
Website: http//blog.daum.net/hanulmoon24

You may purchase individual *Maximum Saints* copies through Amazon.com.
Book One: *Maximum Saints Never Hide in the Dark*
Book Two: *Maximum Saints Make No Little Plans*
Book Three: *Maximum Saints Dream*
Book Four: *Maximum Saints Forgive*
Book Five: *Maximum Saints All Things Are Possible*

Heaven's Gate Ministry (HGM):

Heaven's Gate Ministry reaches out to prisoners, homeless people, hospital patients, and people who have been deported from America to South Korea. HGM also distributes Christian books in prison. For information about how to support this ministry, please contact:

Reverend Lee Born
Heaven's Gate Ministry
Inchon-city, Namdong-gu, Guwol 3-dong, 1888-15
Republic of Korea, Zip code: 405-840
Cell: 010-2210-2504, Office: 070-8278-2504

Email: leeborn777@hanmail.net
Website: http//blog.daum.net/hanulmoon24
          http//blog.daum.net/leeborn777

Veterans Twofish Foundation (VTF)

Veterans Twofish Foundation, a 501(c)(3), non-profit organization, produces, publishes, and distributes stories of veterans and veterans' families. They provide emotional and spiritual support and encouragement to veterans and their families through chaplain's services. Your donation is 100% tax deductible. If you would like to be a partner in this very important mission of reaching out to veterans, or want to know more about this project, please visit them online at: www. veteranstwofish.org, e-mail: veteranstwofish@gmail.com. You may purchase individual copies through Amazon.com.

Veterans Twofish Foundation
P.O. Box 220
Brighton, CO 80601

About The Author

Yong Hui V. McDonald, also known as Vescinda McDonald, is a United Methodist minister, chaplain at Adams County Detention Facility (ACDF) in Brighton, Colorado. She is a certified American Correctional Chaplain, spiritual director and on-call hospital chaplain.

She is the founder of the following:
- Transformation Project Prison Ministry (TPPM), a 501(c)(3) non-profit, in 2005. TPPM produces Maximum Saints books and DVDs of ACDF saints stories of transformation and they are distributed freely to prisons, and homeless shelters.
- GriefPathway Ventures LLC, in 2010, to produce books, DVDs, and audio books to help others to process grief and healing.
- Veterans Twofish Foundation, a 501(c)(3) non-profit, in 2011, to reach out to produce books written by veterans and veterans' families to reach out to other veterans and their families.

Education:
- Multnomah University, B.A.B.E. (1980~1984)
- Iliff School of Theology, Master of Divinity (1999~2002)
- Asbury Theological Seminary student (2013-present)

Books and Audio Books by Yong Hui:

- *Journey With Jesus, Visions, Dreams, Meditations & Reflections*
- *Dancing In The Sky, A Story of Hope for Grieving Hearts*
- *Twisted Logic, The Shadow of Suicide*
- *Twisted Logic, The Window of Depression*
- *Dreams & Interpretations, Healing from Nightmares*
- *I Was The Mountain, In Search of Faith & Revival*
- *The Ultimate Parenting Guide, How to Enjoy Peaceful Parenting and Joyful Children*
- *Prisoners Victory Parade, Extraordinary Stories of Maximum Saints & Former Prisoners*
- *Four Voices, How They Affect Our Mind: How to Overcome Self-Destructive Voices and Hear the Nurturing Voice of God*
- *Tornadoes, Grief, Loss, Trauma, and PTSD: Tornadoes, Lessons and Teachings—The TLT Model for Healing*
- *Prayer and Meditations, 12 Prayer Projects for Spiritual Growth and Healing*
- *Invisible Counselor, Amazing Stories of the Holy Spirit*
- *Tornadoes of Spiritual Warfare, How to Recognize & Defend Yourself From Negative Forces*

- *Tornadoes of Accidents, Finding Peace in Tragic Accidents*
- *Lost But Not Forgotten, Life Behind Prison Walls*
- *Loving God, 100 Daily Meditations and Prayers*
- *Journey With Jesus Two, Visions, Dreams, Meditations & Reflections*
- *Women Who Lead, Stories about Women Who Are Making A Difference*
- Complied and published *Tornadoes of War, Inspirational Stories of Veterans and Veteran's Families* under the Veterans Twofish Foundation.
- Compiled and published five *Maximum Saints* books under the Transformation Project Prison Ministry.

DVDs produced:
- *Dancing In The Sky, Mismatched Shoes*
- *Tears of The Dragonfly, Suicide and Suicide Prevention*

Spanish books:
- *Twisted Logic, The Shadow of Suicide*
- *Journey With Jesus, Visions, Dreams, Meditations and Reflections*

Korean books (한국어로 번역된 책들):

- 『예수님과 걷는 길, 비전, 꿈, 묵상과 회상』
  (*Journey With Jesus, Visions, Dreams, Meditations & Reflections*)
- 『치유, 사랑하는 이들을 잃은 사람들을 위하여』
  (*Dancing In The Sky, A Story of Hope for Grieving Hearts*)
- 『꿈과 해석, 악몽으로부터 치유를 위하여』
  (*Dreams & Interpretations, Healing from Nightmares*)
- 『나는 산이었다, 믿음과 영적 부흥을 찾아서』
  (*I Was The Mountain, In Search of Faith & Revival*)
- 『하나님의 치유를 구하라, 자살의 돌풍에서 치유를 위하여』 (*Twisted Logic, The Shadow of Suicide*)
- 『승리의 행진, 미국 교도소와 문서 선교 회상록』
  (*Prisoners Victory Parade, Extraordinary Stories of Maximum Saints & Former Prisoners*)
- 『네가지 음성, 악한 음성을 저지하고 하나님의 음성을 듣는 영적훈련』 (Four *Voices, How Do They Affect Our Mind*)
- 『하나님 사랑합니다, 100일 묵상과 기도』

(*Loving God, 100 Daily Meditations and Prayers*)

- 『영적 전쟁에서의 승리의 길』 (*Tornadoes of Spiritual Warfare, How to Recognize & Defend Yourself From Negative Forces*)
- 『예수님과 걷는 길 2편, 비전, 꿈, 묵상과 회상』 (*Journey With Jesus Two, Visions, Dreams, Meditations & Reflections*)

About The Illustrator

Holly Weipz, a resident of Brighton Colorado, is a participant of the City of Brighton's Artist on Eye of Art Program. She is a member of St. Augustine Catholic Church and enjoys drawing and painting.